# Contents

# God with us

 I am the new editor of *Daily Bread*. It is a joy and privilege to be asked to take on the role. My first encounter with Scripture Union was at what was then known as a CSSM (Children's Special Service Mission) holiday club in my local park when I was at primary school. I remember those days with fondness and gratitude. I was also a *Daily Bread* reader as a young person and found it invaluable in my discipleship. So SU is not new to me.

I would like to express my appreciation of the wonderful job that Emlyn and 'Tricia have done over the years and I am so pleased that we are not losing them from the *Daily Bread* family as they both hope to be involved in the writing of notes. They have been so helpful to me, encouraging and supporting me as I take on this new role.

This quarter includes Christmas, when we celebrate the birth of Jesus, Emmanuel, God with us. As we come afresh to passages which may be very familiar or very new, we remember that God is with us as we prepare, read, explore and respond and that he leads and guides us as we wonder and ponder our passage for each day.

The reading for Christmas Day is Isaiah 9:1–7 with verse 2 highlighted: 'The people walking in darkness have seen a great light'. As we approach this quarter's readings, let's seek to be aware that God is with us and that we can reflect and share the great light of Jesus that is so needed in our world today.

**Sally Nash**
Editor

# Daily Bread toolbox

**...lly Nash**
...as originally a
...condary school
...acher. She has
...orked in ministry
...nd theological
...ducation for
...any years,
...cluding with
...itish Youth
...r Christ, St
...ohn's College
...ottingham
...nd St Padarn's
...stitute in Cardiff.
...ally enjoys
...riting and has
...ublished a
...nge of books
...nd articles on
...fferent aspects
... ministry,
...cluding work
...ith children and
...oung people.
...he is a practical
...eologian
...ith research
...terests in
...ame, longevity
... ministry and
...aediatric spiritual
...are. Sally is a
...lf-supporting
...ssociate minister
... an outer estate
...urch.

## WAY IN

This page introduces both the notes and the writer. It sets the scene and tells you what you need to know to get into each series.

## A DAY'S NOTE

The notes for each day include five key elements: *Prepare, Read* (the Bible passage for the day), *Explore, Respond* and *Bible in a year.* These are intended to provide a helpful way of meeting God in his Word.

## PREPARE

Prepare yourself to meet with God and pray that the Holy Spirit will help you to understand and respond to what you read.

## READ

Read the Bible passage, taking time to absorb and simply enjoy it. A verse or two from the Bible text is usually included on each page, but it's important to read the whole passage.

## EXPLORE

Explore the meaning of the passage, listening for what God may be saying to you. Before you read the comment, ask yourself: what is the main point of this passage? What is God showing me about himself or about my life? Is there a promise or a command, a warning or example to take special notice of?

## RESPOND

Respond to what God has shown you in the passage in worship and pray for yourself and others. Decide how to share your discoveries with others.

## BIBLE IN A YEAR

If your aim is to know God and his Word more deeply, why not follow this plan and read the whole Bible in one year?

# Long-held values

Have you ever considered what your personal values are? Perhaps you value integrity or honesty. Maybe you're driven by compassion and generosity?

Whatever they may be, your values will undoubtedly shape you and influence the way you live your life.

The same is true for movements like Scripture Union. Just as with individuals, values play an important part in the outworking of a movement and that's why we've recently taken time to stop, consider and reiterate the values that we hold collectively as Scripture Union England and Wales.

As we explored, one thing became immediately clear – the six values that we've now defined (see below) are not new values for Scripture Union. Far from it in fact. Rather, we discovered that the values we hold dear today are values that SU has held for more than 150 years, right since our early days as the Children's Special Services Mission. Whether they've been explicitly articulated over the years or not, the 'new' values are evident in the stories of what God has been doing through SU across the decades.

Perhaps then, you're asking why we are bothering to articulate them now.

Apart from being a good reminder to us all of who we are, we've had the chance to consider how our values are reflected in our actions and behaviours as a movement – does what we do communicate who we are and vice versa? And we've been able to look at the long-held principles of Scripture Union too, to make sure we continue to demonstrate those in our work.

Our heritage is so important to us!

## Scripture Union England and Wales' Values

We have defined six core values that help shape and drive us:

### The Living God

*We serve the living God, depending on him in faith and trusting him to transform us and the lives of those we work with.*

God first. Always. We believe that Scripture Union's mission is God-given, and that we as individuals and as a movement are called to serve and glorify him as we make him known to the 95% of non-churchgoing children and young people in England and Wales ('the 95').

Everything we do is done in, through and for God. As it says in 2 Corinthians 6:16, 'For we are the temple of the living God. As God has said: "I will live with them and walk among them, and I will be their God and they will be my people."'

Day to day, this will be evident in how Scripture Union staff and volunteers approach the work – we ensure that everyone at SU feels called to play their part and can see how the work they do contributes to God's overall mission.

### The Bible

*We are rooted in the Bible, seeking a sound understanding that is applied in daily living and encouraged in the lives of others.*

With a name like Scripture Union, it's probably not a surprise that the Bible is one of our values! It's also key to our overall mission as a movement, which is 'to create opportunities for children and young people to explore the Bible, respond to Jesus and grow in faith'. We don't just want them to hear about Jesus, we want them to encounter him for themselves through the Bible.

When Jesus met some of his earliest followers on the road to Emmaus, even *he* used the scriptures to explain who he was (Luke 24:27), so it makes sense that we would do the same.

Ever since Annie Marston created the Bible cards for children back in the late 1800s, we've been helping children and young people (as well as the not-so-young!) to dig deeper into the Bible and understand it better.

Today, we still publish Bible reading guides – you're reading one of them now – but our key focus is on helping the 95 to engage with Jesus through the Bible.

As a staff team, we meet every day at the beginning of the day to study God's Word together.

We also ensure that all of our resources are rooted in the Bible so that everything we do comes from there.

## SU article

### Prayer

*We trust in the power of prayer, embedding it into everything we do.*

Philippians 4:6 says, 'Do not be anxious about anything, but in every situation, by prayer and petition, with thanksgiving, present your requests to God.' When the Bible tells us to present every situation to God, it is easy to see how that then becomes one of our values. It is a constant reminder for us that we don't work in our own strength, but in God's strength, doing the work that he calls us to do. By bringing all of that to him in prayer, we trust him to guide us as we do it, to provide all that is needed and to use what we offer for his purposes.

When we meet every day to study the Word, we also pray together – for the 95, for the Faith Guides and churches who we partner with, for our supporters, our work and anything else that comes up. We come together to bring everything to God, trusting him with it all. It's also why we include daily prayer requests in *Connecting You*, our quarterly supporter magazine (see su.org.uk/connectingyou to subscribe) and on our online Bible reading guide, Word Live (www.wordlive.org).

### Children and Young People

*We share God's heart for children and young people, demonstrating his love to them and inviting them into a lifelong relationship with Jesus.*

Way back in 1867, as SU's founder Josiah Spiers wrote 'God Is Love' in the sands at Llandudno, the focus of our mission has been children and young people. We believe wholeheartedly that there is no age limit for a relationship with God, and that the youngest generations need to hear and respond to the invitation that God gives, especially today as a staggering 95% don't go to church. In Mark 10:13–16, Jesus makes it quite clear that children are welcome in the kingdom of heaven, and in Matthew 18 we see him exhorting us adults to become more childlike as we receive it. In fact, he goes further than that in warning against anyone who obstructs children in their belief in him (Matthew 18:6,7) and we take that very seriously at Scripture Union.

That's why we work so hard to provide activities, resources, holidays, events and more, all designed to help children and young people get to know Jesus in a way that's appropriate to their age, ability and interests. Our aim is to help them build a faith that lasts a lifetime.

### Responsibility

*We work to create a safe and caring culture in all we do, reflecting God's heart as we strive to excel in the mission he has called us to.*

We believe that God calls us to love one another, and that love extends to how we treat and care for one another. As John writes, 'let us not love with words or speech but with actions and in truth' (1 John 3:18), so we take our responsibilities seriously, making sure that our culture and activities are safe and caring environments for children, young people, volunteers and staff alike. It's why we continue to strive for excellence in our safeguarding policies and practices, complete risk assessments and health and safety audits for all activities, and maintain our first aid and mental health first aid qualifications within the team. It might sound like a lot of training and admin but it's part of our practical outworking of God's love.

### Relationship

*We invest in relationships to advance mission opportunities, equipping and empowering each other in the kingdom.*

We're really excited by our God-given mission to share his good news with the 95, but it's a huge task and not one we can accomplish on our own. That's why we are committed to working in relationship with others: with individuals as Faith Guides or volunteers at events, with churches who share our vision and calling, and with other organisations who also hold this common goal.

It's this unity that we read about in Ephesians 4:15,16, where 'speaking the truth in love, we will grow to become in every respect the mature body of him who is the head, that is, Christ. From him the whole body, joined and held together by every supporting ligament, grows and builds itself up in love, as each part does its work'.

At the time of writing, we're in relationship with hundreds of Faith Guides and their churches, as well as working partnerships with several like-minded Christian organisations.

We hope, as you've read through these six values, that you've seen the SU you know and love in them. It's our prayer that, firstly, we'll already be living out these values as we work and, secondly, we'll continue to grow in each one of them, with God's help.

We're so grateful for your partnership and support as we do. Please continue to pray for SU's work as we demonstrate God's love to the 95 through who we are, how we act and what we say.

---

### Some changes

*Alongside our values, mission and vision, we also have a priority as a movement – reaching those who don't yet know him. We call these children and young people 'the 95' because statistics show that 95% of all under-18s in England and Wales don't go to church. Our digital and print resources are increasingly focused on helping churches reach the 95 and, as such, our* Light *resources (for churches to use with their Sunday Schools) will no longer be available after the end of 2024. This will allow us to focus further on supporting churches in their efforts to reach the 95. Please join us in prayer for our Development Hub as they continue to produce inspiring resources to aid this vital outreach.*

# Joy amid opposition

Philippi was a mixed place. It was a Roman colony, which meant that Roman law ruled in the city. A sprinkling of Roman army veterans had plots of land, among a majority of native Greeks. Perhaps a quarter of the population were Roman citizens. The city had many temples, including for the worship of the emperor, which presented a challenge to people who worshipped Jesus as Lord (Philippians 2:9–11).

### About the writer
**Steve Walton**

Steve Walton is Senior Research Fellow in New Testament of Trinity College, Bristol, and has published widely in New Testament Studies, especially on Luke and Acts. He has taught in colleges and universities in Bedford, Cambridge, London and Nottingham. He is a retired international volleyball referee, and lives with his wife, Ali, and their Border Terrier, Flora.

Paul, Timothy and Silas planted the church there after a vision (Acts 16:9). After initial success in Lydia's conversion (Acts 16:13–15), Paul clashed with the owners of a fortune-telling slave girl after he delivered her from a spirit (Acts 16:16–21). Paul and Silas were freed from prison after a series of incidents and left a small group of believers based in Lydia's home (Acts 16:40).

The Philippian believers had sent financial support to Paul more than once, most recently through Epaphroditus (Philippians 2:25–30; 4:18), and this letter is in part expressing Paul's thanks (4:10,14–19). It is also one of Paul's warmest letters, full of the theme of joy (1:4,18,25; 2:2,17,18,29; 3:1; 4:1,4,10) – this despite the evidence that the believers faced opposition from both Jews and Gentiles (1:27–30; 3:2,18,19).

Why not read the letter through at a sitting to get an overall impression before you dive into the detail? It should take 15–20 minutes.

# Two gospel co-workers

## PREPARE
**Identify where you are in tune with Christ's mindset (Philippians 2:5) and give thanks for what God has done to make you like that.**

............................................................................

## READ
**Philippians 2:19–30**

## EXPLORE
Re-read verses 6–11. In what ways do Timothy's and Epaphroditus' lives show 'the same mindset as Christ Jesus' (2:5)?

Timothy (vs 19–24) is a regular co-worker of Paul. He is son and grandson of godly Jewish women (2 Timothy 1:5), and his father was Greek (Acts 16:1). Paul had Timothy circumcised so that he would be acceptable in evangelism in Jewish circles (Acts 16:3). Paul often sends him to prepare for a visit or to see how a church is doing in Paul's absence (v 19; eg 1 Corinthians 4:17; 16:10; 1 Thessalonians 3:1–2,6). Timothy's readiness to focus on Christ's interests, rather than his own, is central to his work (v 21).

Epaphroditus is sent by the Philippians to support Paul (v 25), but has become very ill (vs 26,27,30). Probably Epaphroditus was the bearer of money to support Paul during his Roman imprisonment.

Paul appreciates him, describing him very positively (v 25). However, illness has prevented Epaphroditus from serving Paul as the Philippians had hoped. Nevertheless, Paul does not want his hearers to see him as a failure, and so speaks warmly of him and calls the believers to honour him (v 29). Paul recognises Epaphroditus' readiness to serve even at great cost to himself.

In your relationships with one another, have the same mindset as Christ Jesus.

**Philippians 2:5**

---

## RESPOND
Give thanks to God for those in your church who serve in the background, like these two, putting Christ's interests first at cost to themselves.

............................................................................

**Bible in a year:** Isaiah 61,62; Hebrews 12

# Wednesday 2 October
Philippians 3:1–11

# Where's your confidence?

## PREPARE
What do you have to rejoice about (v 1)? Write a list and spend time being joyful before the Lord.

## READ
**Philippians 3:1–11**

## EXPLORE
'Confidence' is a key word here (vs 3,4). Paul's confidence had been in his heritage as a Jew, a learned, law-observant Pharisee and a persecutor of the Jesus-followers (vs 5,6). Some think of Paul as deeply burdened by guilt before he met Jesus on the road to Damascus (Acts 9:1–19), but his reflection here is that as far as right standing with God under the Jewish law was concerned, he was faultless (v 6).

Paul warns the Philippians about people who sought to persuade Gentile believers to keep the Jewish law and (for men) accept circumcision (v 2; we meet these people in Galatians, too). It could be tempting, for Judaism was an established way of life, so Gentile believers could avoid being treated so much as social outsiders if others saw them as Jewish.

Against this pressure, Paul focuses the believers' attention afresh on Jesus.

Verses 7–11 are one long sentence in Greek, drawing a contrast, but not between 'Christianity' and 'Judaism', for Paul is still deeply Jewish. It is about finding that what God freely gives through Jesus is more valuable than all things – for Jesus makes us God's own people.

Note down the things which flow from trusting Christ (vs 7–11) and give thanks to God for them.

> But whatever were gains to me I now consider loss for the sake of Christ.
>
> **Philippians 3:7**

## RESPOND
Search for a YouTube recording of Graham Kendrick's song 'Knowing you, Jesus' (2011), based on this passage, and listen worshipfully to it.

**Bible in a year:** Isaiah 63,64; Hebrews 13

# Press on!

## PREPARE

Who has helped you grow in the Christian life? Make a list of key people and thank God for them.

........................................................................

## READ

**Philippians 3:12–21**

## EXPLORE

Paul portrays dynamic and forward-facing Christian maturity. He isn't complacent about where he stands as a Jesus-follower now, but focuses on what Christ has done, is doing and will do – and his own response. Christ has 'taken hold' of Paul (v 12), and Paul responds by pressing on to the finish line. In the Roman games, the victor went into the crowd to the president of the games to receive their victory laurel wreath – but in Paul's case it is God's call to a heavenly reward (v 14).

Christ will return at the last day and complete the work he began in believers' lives, transforming them in every way to be what he intends (vs 20,21). Jesus' glorious resurrection body is the prototype for our future bodies (v 21) – that's a prospect to look forward to!

So in the present, Christ is to be the focus of the Philippians' attention, not earthly concerns (v 19). This isn't an invitation to abandon this world, but rather to be different *in* this world, showing that we are citizens of another place by our lifestyle (v 20). The believers had learned this model from Paul and Timothy, who planted the church there (v 17; 1:1), and need to persist in copying their model.

> But our citizenship is in heaven. And we eagerly await a Saviour from there, the Lord Jesus Christ.
>
> **Philippians 3:20**

## RESPOND

Reflect on life in the world to come and rejoice in the transformation which Christ will complete in your life at that time.

........................................................................

**Bible in a year:** Isaiah 65,66;  John 1

# Friday 4 October
## Philippians 4:1–9

# Keep your focus!

## PREPARE
What have you thought about most in the past 24 hours? Make a list and evaluate it against verse 8 in today's reading.

. . . . . . . . . . . . . . . . . . . . . . . . . . . . . . . . . . . . . . . . . . . . . . . . . . . . . . . .

## READ
**Philippians 4:1–9**

## EXPLORE
People fell out in Philippi, as today. Paul calls two female leaders, Euodia and Syntyche, to be reconciled (v 2). He also calls on 'my true companion' to help them reconcile (v 3) – maybe a particular person, or a way of referring to the whole congregation. This united mind is a key theme (see 2:2,5; 3:15), expressed by united rejoicing and gentleness – the exhortations are addressed to 'you' plural (vs 4,5).

Unity of mind stems from a shared focus of attention. It's easy to put problems and evil front and centre, but Paul calls us collectively to put good things there (v 8). There are things in the world with these qualities – Paul is not talking only about the church's life: it's 'whatever' (v 8, five times). A great piece of music or art, a brilliant article, an entertaining show, an example of love, a generous gift, all speak of God's love. How might you focus more on such things?

Paul wants the believing community to enjoy God's peace, like a troop of soldiers standing guard on their thinking and acting (v 7). This peace comes by rejoicing, praying and giving thanks (v 6). A church noticeboard said: 'Why pray when you can worry?' – a truth to take notice of!

> Do not be anxious about anything, but in every situation, by prayer and petition, with thanksgiving, present your requests to God.
>
> **Philippians 4:6**

## RESPOND
Where do you need to be gentle with others? Make this a feature of your prayers over the coming week.

. . . . . . . . . . . . . . . . . . . . . . . . . . . . . . . . . . . . . . . . . . . . . . . . . . . . . . . .

**Bible in a year:** Jeremiah 1,2;  Psalms 112,113

# Being content

## PREPARE
**What is your biggest highlight of this letter so far? Re-read it, reflect and rejoice in what God has shown you.**

. . . . . . . . . . . . . . . . . . . . . . . . . . . . . . . . . . . . . . . . . . . . . . . . . . . .

## READ
**Philippians 4:10–23**

## EXPLORE
Verse 13 is often wrongly used to claim that we can do anything we like with God's strength. This interpretation is part of the expressive individualism rife in Western society: life is about *me* and what *I* want – no one can tell me what to do or question my choices.

Here, however, Paul gives thanks without using the words. He refers to their 'renewed … concern' (v 10), their gifts sent with Epaphroditus (vs 15,16,18). Paul uses a series of accountancy phrases to speak of these gifts: 'giving and receiving', 'credited to your account', 'full payment' (vs 15,17,18). He uses these terms subversively to undermine what would be expected in the ancient world: if you sent a gift to someone, they were in your debt and owed you honour or a return gift. Paul is clear that he looks to God with thanks for their gift, using sacrificial imagery (v 18), and that he is not in their debt. Rather, God will give them the return gift to meet their needs (v 19).

Verse 13, then, comes amid Paul explaining that he has learned contentment in good and bad circumstances (vs 11,12). It's God's strength which enables him to keep going, a strength experienced partly through the Philippians' gifts (v 14).

… I have learned to be content whatever the circumstances.

**Philippians 4:11**

## RESPOND
How do you financially support gospel ministry in your community and more widely in your country and the world? Review your giving to consider if you might give more or differently.

. . . . . . . . . . . . . . . . . . . . . . . . . . . . . . . . . . . . . . . . . . . . . . . . . . . .

**Bible in a year:** Jeremiah 3,4;  John 2

## Sunday 6 October
Psalm 7

# God of justice

## PREPARE

Give thanks to God that he is just and will act justly to save and defend his people. Look forward to Jesus' return, when God's justice will be fully seen, and rejoice in that hope.

........................................................................

## READ
**Psalm 7**

## EXPLORE

It's hard having untrue rumours put about by opponents. That's the world this psalm assumes (vs 1–5), a world familiar today in politics or work or (alas, sometimes) church. Although we do not know Cush (in the psalm's title), we do know that some Benjaminites refused to have David as king (2 Samuel 20:1,2). What to do?

David turns to God for justice (vs 6–11). Judges in Israel both decided cases and took the required action which followed, and that's the basis of David's appeal to God. He asks God as judge to vindicate him publicly in the divine court where God is enthroned (v 7), and to make the wicked stop acting this way (v 9).

David does not plan how to deal with his opponents himself – that's God's problem. Like Paul, he leaves God to act, rather than acting himself (Romans 12:19,20,

echoing Proverbs 25:21,22). If his opponents don't back off (v 12), God will prepare powerful weapons to enforce justice (vs 12b,13). These people's violence will come back on their own heads as God acts (vs 14–16). So David confidently praises God because he knows God will act justly (v 17).

> My shield is God Most High,
> who saves the upright in heart.
> **Psalm 7:10**

## RESPOND
Pray for people being slandered or publicly attacked, especially Christian leaders, that they will put their hope in God and that God will vindicate them.

........................................................................

**Bible in a year:** Jeremiah 5,6;  John 3

# Bound for freedom

In my years of running Scripture Union children's holidays, I twice used the story of Moses and the Exodus as the main theme. For me, the passage we begin these readings with was always central: the Passover. On one occasion, we made a doorframe and used red paint to mark it, then moved the posts together and the lintel down to represent the cross. I remember the children being moved, and 'getting it'. Several of our readings cover events of the Old Testament prefiguring the New.

Both times, we ended with the crossing of the Red Sea and the triumph over the Egyptians. Up to that point, the readings are full of God's plan and God's power: his plan to redeem his people and his power over the enemy. So far, so victorious.

What we didn't do was take the story any further into the desert. What comes over clearly in the final few readings is how fickle God's people were, how quickly they complained, how quickly they forgot what the Lord had done and how ready they were to abandon his plan. As well as that though, the graciousness and patience of God as they moaned and grumbled are evident.

As we reconnect with these Old Testament events and see how their impact still has relevance for us, I pray that this series will encourage you in God as he frees and provides for his people, then and now.

About the writer
**Gill Robertson**

Gill is a 60-something recently retired vicar's wife, step-mother, fairly new grandmother and a carer. She is also a Lay Reader (LLM), musician, composer, crafter and cook; and the time spent on these activities is inversely proportional to that spent on housework!

# Monday 7 October
## Exodus 12:1–13

# The way to freedom

**PREPARE**
**Think about the preaching and teaching where you worship. How often is an Old Testament passage the subject of choice for a reading or a sermon series? Or is the New Testament where the focus is? Does it matter?**

................................................................

**READ**
**Exodus 12:1–13**

**EXPLORE**
Getting to the first floor of a house without passing through the ground floor is tricky, but not impossible. Watching a play beginning with Act 2 would give you some understanding of the plot, but not a full one.

This passage – as so much of the Old Testament – acts like the ground floor, or Act 1. It is fundamental to us having a richer, deeper appreciation of Jesus in the New Testament. The lamb chosen for the Passover meal had to be without defect (v 5). The blood smeared on the doorposts and lintels of their houses protected all inside from death (v 13). The Passover precipitated the Israelites' journey from slavery to the freedom of the Promised Land.

The many lambs of the Passover point us towards Jesus, the only Lamb of God (eg John 1:29; 1 Peter 1:19). He was without sin (eg Hebrews 4:15). His blood redeems us and offers us forgiveness (eg Ephesians 1:7). His death opens up the way to freedom from the slavery of sin into the new life of the kingdom of God (eg Romans 6:18).

'... and when I see the blood, I will pass over you.'

**Exodus 12:13**

**RESPOND**
Redemption; forgiveness; freedom; new life. Give thanks to God for all that Jesus, the Lamb of God, makes possible in our lives.

................................................................

**Bible in a year:** Jeremiah 7,8;  Psalms 114,115

# Make the memorial

## PREPARE
What special occasions do you celebrate in your family? How do you celebrate them? Do you have any that are personal to you? Why do you think remembering and celebrating are important?

......................................................................................

## READ
**Exodus 12:14–30**

## EXPLORE
As well as repeating the instructions for what the Israelites must do with the blood of the lamb (vs 21–23), Moses tells them that what will happen that night is something that must be remembered and celebrated for generations to come; it must be commemorated every year from then on. Their children (and all those to come) must know the importance of what happened. And the details are so important that there is a severe penalty if they aren't observed (v 19).

This passage too has ground floor/ Act 1 significance. It's at the Passover meal with his disciples (found in all four Gospels) that Jesus tells them to break bread and drink wine in remembrance of him. This became a practice right after the resurrection (Acts 2:42), and Paul elaborates on what to do and how to do it (and not do it) in 1 Corinthians 11. However we follow Jesus' command

to remember him, and celebrate our salvation, its practice is right at the heart of who we are as his people.

> 'Celebrate this day as a lasting ordinance for the generations to come.'
> **Exodus 12:17**

## RESPOND
Eucharist (thanksgiving); Communion; breaking of bread; mass (sending out); the Lord's Supper; an agape (the love seen on the cross) meal. Which of the meanings behind these names for the memorial of Jesus' death have significance for you, and why?

......................................................................................

**Bible in a year:** Jeremiah 9,10; John 4

# Wednesday 9 October
## Exodus 12:31–42

# Who's in charge?

## PREPARE
Some events in our lives can bring about dramatic change. They might be joyful, full of sadness, or unexpectedly left field. How has your life changed because of specific circumstances?

. . . . . . . . . . . . . . . . . . . . . . . . . . . . . . . . . . . . . . . . . . . . . . . . . . . .

## READ
**Exodus 12:31–42**

## EXPLORE
For the first nine plagues, Pharaoh either refused outright to let the Israelites go, or stipulated particular conditions under which they could leave. Each time his heart was hardened and when the plague ceased he changed his mind and the Israelites stayed put. And despite all that, several times he requested Moses to pray to the Lord for him. (Glance through Exodus 7–11.)

This time, the final plague, with its catastrophic deathly outcome, tips Pharaoh into letting the Israelites go for long enough for them to actually leave. Indeed, he's in a big hurry for them to leave. So are the Egyptians (v 33). Everything the Israelites need, he grants. And he still wants their blessing (vs 31,32). The Israelites are able to take advantage of this situation and come away materially provided for (vs 35,36) as well as with food for the beginning of the journey.

Above all, this is the hand of the Lord. It is his doing that the Israelites leave with such riches (v 36). And it is his watchfulness that allows the Exodus finally to begin (v 42).

## 'Up! Leave my people, you and the Israelites!'
**Exodus 12:31**

## RESPOND
What circumstances are you, or your loved ones, facing? Give thanks today that in all of them, the Lord is watching over us and is acting for our good.

. . . . . . . . . . . . . . . . . . . . . . . . . . . . . . . . . . . . . . . . . . . . . . . . . . . .

**Bible in a year:** Jeremiah 11,12;  John 5

# In or out

## PREPARE

An experience of exclusion from a group you want to belong to can be upsetting. Have you ever felt excluded from a group of people? For what reason? How did the situation resolve?

........................................................

## READ

**Exodus 12:43–51**

## EXPLORE

God's instructions to Moses and Aaron for how the Passover meal must happen don't leave any wiggle room. In addition to eating it inside, it's striking that the bones of the lamb must remain whole (v 46). Here is another example of something in the Old Testament pointing towards something in the New. Breaking the bones of a crucified criminal was common, as it hastened death. But this did not happen to Jesus, who had already finished the work of the cross and given up his spirit before the soldiers came to do it (see John 19:30–37).

The Passover was also to be inclusive of all who underwent circumcision. Any foreigner who was prepared to be circumcised could be included just like those 'born in the land' (v 48). As long as all the males in the family were circumcised, they counted as native. In Deuteronomy 10 and 30, Moses reminds the people that circumcision is not just a physical matter. It applies to everyone and concerns the heart. Paul takes this up in Romans 2:28,29: the work of the Spirit on and in our hearts is what matters.

'The same law applies both to the native-born and to the foreigner residing among you.'

**Exodus 12:49**

## RESPOND

From a human perspective, inclusion seems to be about being accepted for who we are. From God's perspective, inclusion – for anyone – is about Jesus (John 14:6).

........................................................

**Bible in a year:** Jeremiah 13,14;  John 6

## Friday 11 October
### Exodus 13:1–16

# Redemption

## PREPARE

**I am the eldest of my siblings. Before I was born, my mother prayed as Hannah prayed in 1 Samuel 1:11 (not the razor bit!) and gave me back to God. How does your church celebrate new birth?**

............................................................................

## READ
### Exodus 13:1–16

## EXPLORE

In this passage, the importance of remembering and celebrating the Israelites' freedom from Egypt has a particular context: the consecration of the firstborn. Being the firstborn, the one who inherited the double portion and the father's name, was already significant; the transaction between Esau and Jacob is an example of this (Genesis 25:27–34). The Passover itself indicates this too. It was the firstborn son of both humans and animals that died. Now, God says, every firstborn male, human and animal, was to be seen as belonging to God. Firstborn animals were to be sacrificed (with one exception); firstborn sons were to be redeemed by sacrificing a lamb (vs 12,13). Every time this happened it was to serve as a reminder of the power and might of the Lord (v 16).

Once more, this points us forward to the Lamb of God. Jesus offers everyone redemption from the slavery of sin through the sacrifice of his own life (1 Peter 1:18,19). Each of us is redeemed with his precious blood. And each of us is worthy of redemption.

> 'You are to give over to the LORD the first offspring of every womb.'
>
> **Exodus 13:12**

## RESPOND

What should our response be? 'Therefore, I urge you, brothers and sisters, in view of God's mercy, to offer your bodies as a living sacrifice, holy and pleasing to God – this is your true and proper worship' (Romans 12:1). Pray through what this means for you today.

............................................................................

**Bible in a year:** Jeremiah 15,16;  Psalm 116

# The way to go

**PREPARE**
How have you experienced God's guidance in your life? Have there been any completely unexpected occasions that really surprised you? Give thanks for the way he has led you.

........................................................................................

**READ**
**Exodus 13:17–22**

**EXPLORE**
Despite the Israelites being ready in case of opposition (v 18), God shows great care for his people in the way he led them. He knows what they could cope with and what might be too much for them. So although the route is longer, he takes them towards the Red (or Reed) Sea. And he enables travel at any time of day or night. Imagine the feelings of the Israelites as they saw the pillar of cloud or the pillar of fire, signifying the Lord's presence with them, going ahead. Imagine how, after so long crying out to God for deliverance (Exodus 2:23–25), the whole experience of God in action – through the plagues, the Passover and now the journey away from Egypt – has affected them. I wonder what it made them think about God himself.

There's a hint in there – 'they might change their minds' (v 17) – about the fickleness of God's people, which we'll see more of in the readings to come. But for now, there's no choice about which way to go – it's plainly obvious. They're going God's way.

> So God led the people around by the desert road towards the Red Sea.
>
> **Exodus 13:18**

**RESPOND**
Guidance from the Lord comes in so many ways. Sometimes, it might well be spectacular. More often, it's not. What's certain is that he will guide us. Bring to God today whatever you need him to guide you in.

........................................................................................

**Bible in a year:** Jeremiah 17,18;  John 7

## Sunday 13 October
Psalm 8

# God and us

## PREPARE

'Join with all nature in manifold witness to thy great faithfulness, mercy and love' (Thomas Chisholm, 1923). Use this or another hymn or worship song to come before God today.

. . . . . . . . . . . . . . . . . . . . . . . . . . . . . . . . . . . . . . . . . . . . . . . . . . . . . . . . . . . . . . . . . . .

## READ
**Psalm 8**

## EXPLORE

I and a few friends once spent several hours on a very mild, clear November evening somewhere up on Dartmoor in Devon. We stopped to gaze at the stars. There was no light pollution and the longer we looked up into the night sky the further into the heavens it seemed we could see. More stars became visible and the immensity of space seemed both vast and very close. It was a wonderful experience.

In this psalm, David expresses that awe and wonder in direct praise to God. The majesty and power of the Lord is extolled. It leads David to ask, 'Why do you bother with us?' (v 4, *The Message*). It seems overwhelming to him that the Lord should be mindful of us and care for us.

Having seen the power of God acting on their behalf, Moses and the Israelites might have answered that question differently – but they stood, and we now stand, in awe of the name of the Lord, and in awe that he knows and loves us.

## You have set your glory in the heavens.
**Psalm 8:1**

## RESPOND
We have let God down in the responsibility of caring for the earth and all its inhabitants (vs 5–8). What opportunities do you (or your church) have to encourage people to care for the earth, not just because it's a good thing to do but because it's God's creation?

. . . . . . . . . . . . . . . . . . . . . . . . . . . . . . . . . . . . . . . . . . . . . . . . . . . . . . . . . . . . . . . . . . .

**Bible in a year:** Jeremiah 19,20; John 8

# Who's in charge?

## PREPARE

As a teenager, I had a go-to song to sing in my head at difficult times, to encourage myself in God. It ended with the reminder that in Christ we are more than conquerors. What helps you in such times?

## READ

**Exodus 14:1–18**

## EXPLORE

This passage has three main characters: Pharaoh, Moses and God.

Pharaoh has been informed of the Israelites' departure (v 5). He galvanises his considerable army into action and chases after the Israelites to re-enslave them. They quickly catch up with them. This understandably terrifies the Israelites. They make the first of their 'We should have stayed in our captivity!' complaints (vs 10–12). From marching along with confidence (v 8), they've immediately changed their minds about their situation.

Moses, therefore, is dealing with them. His confidence in what God will do, as he speaks to the frightened people, is wonderful (vs 13,14); he believes utterly that the Lord is in control. His conviction that the Lord will do a wonderful thing shines out.

And God? God planned it like this (vs 1–4). The confrontation between Israel's God and the gods of Egypt, already seen in the plagues, is now about to culminate in the final overthrow of Pharaoh's army. His instructions to Moses (vs 15–18) are clear and show that this is all about God gaining glory and renown.

'The LORD will fight for you; you need only to be still.'

**Exodus 14:14**

## RESPOND

It can be really hard, in the middle of sudden, frightening or upsetting situations, to keep our focus on the Lord and wait for his deliverance. Pray for anyone known to you who needs 'only to be still'.

**Bible in a year:** Jeremiah 21,22; Psalms 117,118

Exodus 14:19–31

# Trust and obey

## PREPARE
Have you ever faced active hostility because of your faith? What happened? What was the outcome? How did the Lord help you?

. . . . . . . . . . . . . . . . . . . . . . . . . . . . . . . . . . . . . . . . . . . . . . . . . . . . . . . . . . . . . . . . .

## READ
**Exodus 14:19–31**

## EXPLORE
God's care and protection over his people in this passage is clear. First, the cloud moves and positions itself between the two opposing forces. It provides light for God's people and darkness for the Egyptians, effectively keeping them apart during the night (vs 19,20). Then the Lord causes the wind to blow so strongly that a pathway through the waters is created, leading the people to freedom on the other side (vs 21,22).

The Egyptian army, chasing after their fleeing workforce, get confused by what's going on. Their chariot wheels jam, they decide to get away from the Israelites, and they realise – belatedly – the power of the God of the Israelites (vs 23–25). But it's too late. The sea flows back as Moses follows God's command and the whole army perishes (vs 26–28). The Egyptians who wanted to drown Hebrew baby boys are now drowned themselves.

End result (v 31)? The Israelites have had a dramatic demonstration of exactly what their God can do. The passage is dominated by what the Lord does. This fills them with awe at who God is, as well as causing them to trust him and the person he has called and chosen to lead them: Moses.

That day the LORD saved Israel from the hands of the Egyptians, and Israel saw the Egyptians lying dead on the shore.

**Exodus 14:30**

## RESPOND
Look back through all of chapter 14 for the phrases that indicate what the Lord did in rescuing his people. What situations are you facing? Pray with confidence and trust.

. . . . . . . . . . . . . . . . . . . . . . . . . . . . . . . . . . . . . . . . . . . . . . . . . . . . . . . . . . . . . . . . .

**Bible in a year:** Jeremiah 23,24;  John 9

# Time to rejoice

## PREPARE
Use any favourite hymn or song to praise the Lord as you come into his presence today.

........................................................

## READ
**Exodus 15:1–21**

## EXPLORE
This passage can be considered as the first psalm in the Bible. It repeats in poetic form the events the Israelites have just been through. It celebrates the total triumph of God over their enemy (vs 1–12). It looks ahead to other surrounding nations feeling subdued because of this and leaving them alone (vs 14–16) and prophesies what God will do in settling and establishing the people (vs 13,17).

The emotion of the occasion is evident in the singing and dancing, in which both men and women take the lead. It's an exuberant outpouring of joy and praise that places God at the centre of all that has happened. He is the one who has accomplished the victory, and verse 11 rightly says that no other god is like their God or can do what their God can.

Who wouldn't be emotional after all they have experienced? If we think of the rollercoaster of tension and fear, anticipation, excitement and relief, and further back through all the years of oppression, it's not surprising that, now they are finally free, their feelings explode into this celebration of God, his character and his works.

'The LORD is my strength and my defence; he has become my salvation.'

**Exodus 15:2**

## RESPOND
When life is good, praise flows; when it's hard, praise can be difficult. Whatever your circumstances are, focus on the Lord and what he has done in your life. God is always worthy of our praise.

........................................................

**Bible in a year:** Jeremiah 25,26;  John 10

# Thursday 17 October

Exodus 15:22–27

# First hurdle

## PREPARE

**Have you experienced a time when what God wanted you to do seemed really difficult? Did you do it or not? Either way, what was the outcome?**

## READ

**Exodus 15:22–27**

## EXPLORE

Up to now, the Israelites have been travelling away from Egypt, fleeing their enemy and seeing God do miraculous things. Now the journey towards the Promised Land begins. It doesn't start well. In spite of Exodus 14:31, adverse conditions quickly lead the people to complain, against Moses particularly. Clearly, it's Moses' fault that they're thirsty.

Three days without water in dry and dusty conditions is hard to live through. The water at Marah must have seemed a wonderful sight until they tried to drink it. Jamie Buckingham,* a frequent traveller in that region, suggests that, had they been able to drink the water, the minerals would have purged them of the internal parasites and diseases they brought with them from Egypt and helped them cope with the hot weather. But this first test was too much. Moses cries out to God, a way is found for the water to become drinkable, and God makes one of his 'If... then...' conditional promises (v 26). Will they listen?

> There the LORD issued a ruling and instruction for them and put them to the test.
>
> **Exodus 15:25**

## RESPOND

It's not easy to face up to the idea that sometimes what God wants us to do is going to be hard in some way. All of what he asks of us has his plan and purpose behind it; pray for anyone you know who is facing difficult decisions.

*J Buckingham, *A Way through the Wilderness*, Risky Living Ministries, Inc, 2013

**Bible in a year:** Jeremiah 27,28; John 11

# Bread of heaven

## PREPARE
What circumstances have you been in that made trusting in the Lord seem a really hard thing to do? How did things turn out?

..........................................................................

## READ
**Exodus 16:1–16**

## EXPLORE
After the refreshment of the 12 springs at Elim, the Israelites are fully engaged on their desert journey. It's still not going well. The food they could bring with them from Egypt (see Exodus 12:34–39) is all gone and the hardships of Egypt have been forgotten. The pots of meat they had there dominate their thinking – and presumably they'd rather have died full than empty (v 3)! The hungry people easily forgot what God had done and had to be reminded that they were grumbling against God (v 8).

God's plan provided meat (migrating quail) and bread. He came among the people (v 10) and promised to feed them – and he fed them generously (v 16). It's interesting to see that this too is intended as a test for the Israelites (vs 4,5).

It's sad to see how quickly their circumstances make the Israelites change their minds about the Lord. From being their deliverer, someone worthy of great praise, they're now wishing they were dead by his hand (v 3). And how encouraging it is to see that, despite their grumbling and complaining, God acts with grace and mercy towards them.

'Then you will know that I am the LORD your God.'
**Exodus 16:12**

## RESPOND
Pray today for anyone who finds it hard to see how God can be in their circumstances, or who finds it hard to trust him in difficulties. Ask God to show his grace and mercy to them.

..........................................................................

**Bible in a year:** Jeremiah 29–31;  Psalm 119:1–24

Exodus 16:17–30

# God's way or my way

## PREPARE
'Trust and obey, for there's no other way to be happy in Jesus...' (JH Sammis, 1887). What has been your experience of doing this?

· · · · · · · · · · · · · · · · · · · · · · · · · · · · · · · · · · · · · · · · · · · · · · · · · · · · · · · · · · · · · · · ·

## READ
**Exodus 16:17–30**

## EXPLORE
The test God gives the Israelites here is about whether they will follow his commands or their own inclinations concerning the manna. They are supposed to gather enough for each day and not keep any overnight. Some of them keep it overnight and it goes off quickly (vs 19,20). Then, when they can gather twice as much and keep half overnight for the Sabbath, some of them still go and look for it (vs 22–27).

This is both disobedience to God's commands and shows a lack of trust in him. Some of the people didn't do what he asked, and they didn't trust him to keep on providing for their needs. They failed the test. And they continued to fail and God continued to provide. He provided manna right up until they could celebrate the Passover for the first time in Canaan (Joshua 5:10–12).

What God was doing, in providing manna for them to eat for so long, was so important that it had to be saved and preserved in a jar as a reminder to the people of how God cared for them in the wilderness (16:32–34). It was a sign of his commitment to them.

Then the LORD said to Moses, 'How long will you refuse to keep my commands and my instructions?'

**Exodus 16:28**

## RESPOND
Why do you think some of the Israelites found it hard to follow God's command? How would you encourage someone who was struggling to do what God wanted them to do? Is there someone you could encourage today?

· · · · · · · · · · · · · · · · · · · · · · · · · · · · · · · · · · · · · · · · · · · · · · · · · · · · · · · · · · · · · · · ·

**Bible in a year:** Jeremiah 32,33; John 12

# The safest place to be

## PREPARE
'I shall not fear the battle if thou art by my side' (John Bode, 1869). Use this or another hymn or worship song as you come to God today.

........................................................................

## READ
**Psalm 9**

## EXPLORE
David alternates in this psalm between praise and thanksgiving to God for who he is and what he has done (vs 1,2,7–12) and describing the danger and threat he has gone through which the Lord has rescued him from (vs 3–6,13–20). David's trust in the Lord is declared (vs 9,10) and he asks for rescue so that he can rejoice in God (vs 13,14).

The Israelites could have identified with this psalm too. Verses 3–5 can easily be applied to what happened when the Egyptian army tried to reclaim them from freedom back to slavery, and the heartfelt praises of God are echoed in the song of Moses and Miriam (Exodus 15:1).

Whatever enemies we may be facing – enemies without and within – our prayer can be the same as David's: 'Have mercy and lift me up' (v 13) and our confidence and hope is in the Lord who will never forget us (v 18). Our names are written on his hands (Isaiah 49:16) and our lives are hidden with Christ in God (Colossians 3:3).

The LORD is a refuge for the oppressed, a stronghold in times of trouble.

**Psalm 9:9**

---

## RESPOND
Being in any kind of danger is a knee-trembling, stomach-clenching experience. Pray today for anyone known to you in such a situation. Pray that they will know the surrounding presence of the Lord as a refuge and a stronghold.

........................................................................

**Bible in a year:** Jeremiah 34,35; John 13

# The edge of glory

## About the writer
### Rachel Butler

Rachel has taught English in various places around the world, and now lives in Birmingham with her husband, son and step-daughters. She enjoys adventuring in the outdoors and sharing food as often as possible.

Having just been hailed as king by a passionate crowd on the busy streets of Jerusalem, Jesus is now preparing his confused disciples for his death. Chapters 13–16 of John are often known as the 'Book of Glory': Jesus' dense, intricate monologues are only occasionally interspersed with the disciples' questions or symbolic narrative. Sometimes the language feels like a whirlpool, pulling us around repeated rich and deep theological themes: glory, love and witness.

Tradition holds that the author is John the disciple. Irenaeus claims this in AD 180, but whether the 'beloved disciple' (see 21:20,24) is an eyewitness as well as a literary device is debated. The text gives testimony to Jesus in line with, but stylistically distinct from, the Gospels of Matthew, Mark and Luke. It is certainly produced by an evangelist who is aware of the reader's spiritual needs.

Some sections may remain hard to fathom: try reading these out loud, or you could write down questions as you go. I pray that by the end of the next two weeks of Bible reading you will feel more confident in understanding Jesus' relationship with the Father, why he came to earth and what it means to 'believe in Jesus' today. Keep the text's overall purpose in mind. The writer is presenting us with these words so that 'by believing you may have life in his name' (20:31).

# Now is the time

## PREPARE
Pray: 'Holy Spirit, please bring light to my mind and my heart as I seek to understand better who Jesus was and is.'

................................................................

## READ
**John 12:20–36**

## EXPLORE
This passage is a structural turning point in John. The focus shifts from signs or miracles of Jesus (chapters 1–13) to his glorification (chapters 13–16). The Greeks' request, 'we would like to see Jesus' (v 21), sets in motion the ultimate expression of the glory of God that has been anticipated and prophesied.

Jesus' words, 'the hour has come' (v 23), mark and declare this moment's deep significance. He already knows the eternal story that will be revealed by the following scenes. *Now is the time* for Jesus to be glorified. What does 'glorified' mean here (v 23)?

Glory is a repeated theme in John, first introduced in 1:14. Ideas of magnificence, royal majesty and honour help me visualise it. The glory of God in the Old Testament was seen visibly, for example, through the cloud that covered Mount Sinai when Moses received the Ten Commandments (Exodus 24:15,16) or through fire (Deuteronomy 5:24). This is reflected in Jesus' reference to himself as light (vs 35,36).

'Glorified' (vs 23,28) also refers to the specific sequence of events by which Jesus will bring glory to God: the humiliating journey to the cross followed by the resurrection. Jesus is preparing both himself and his disciples for his own death (v 33): a death that brings them and us life (vs 24,32).

Jesus replied, 'The hour has come for the Son of Man to be glorified.'

**John 12:23**

## RESPOND
Do you identify with the crowd's confusion and questions about who Jesus is (v 34) or has this passage helped you understand him more?

................................................................

**Bible in a year:** Jeremiah 36,37;  Psalm 119:25–48

# Not everyone believes

## PREPARE
**What does believing in Jesus mean to you today?**

........................................................

## READ
**John 12:37–50**

## EXPLORE
Let's start by exploring verses 44–50. Jesus speaks with passion (v 44) as he takes his listeners through some key themes: the relationship between the Father and the Son; light and darkness; judgement and eternal life. How are we responding to Jesus' words?

In the intense clarity of verse 45, what is Jesus saying about the nature of his relationship with the Father and how does this connect to verse 41? The familiar themes of light (v 46; see 12:23) and glory (v 41) help us see that believing in Jesus means symbolically coming out of darkness – the darkness of not believing in God or realising that Jesus is a light to show us who God is.

In verses 37–43, John demonstrates that even having seen signs, not everyone will believe in Jesus (vs 38,40). Others believe but don't want anyone else to know (vs 42,43). Jesus knows that not everyone will keep his words (v 47) and that some will reject him (v 48): negative responses (v 42) aren't confirmation that what Jesus says about himself is untrue. There will be judgement on the last day (v 48), but his purpose for being in the world is to speak what the Father commands (v 49), to bring light (v 46) and to save (v 47).

'The one who looks at me is seeing the one who sent me.'
**John 12:45**

## RESPOND
Maybe, like me, you are left mulling over the tricky question of *why* God hardens people's hearts. Take some time to process this question in the light of today's reading.

........................................................

**Bible in a year:** Jeremiah 38,39;  John 14

# Wednesday 23 October
John 13:1–17

# Humble love

## PREPARE
Read Philippians 2:5–11 and meditate on just one or two words that help you to reflect on the unique character of Jesus.

. . . . . . . . . . . . . . . . . . . . . . . . . . . . . . . . . . . . . . . . . . . . . . . . .

## READ
John 13:1–17

## EXPLORE
Embedded in Jesus' extended discourses is this refreshing piece of drama. The disciples recline at the evening meal (v 2). We can imagine a bewildered silence as they watch Jesus get up from the meal (v 4); we hear Peter burst on to the scene with his mix of passion and confusion (vs 8,9). This foot-washing is not the hygienic and practical act of hospitality you might receive on entering a house, but is taking place, bewilderingly, in the middle of the meal.

Verses 1–4 provide a lens through which to view Jesus' purposeful actions. He stoops – literally and symbolically – to take the place of a servant. He can do this without any fear of powerlessness because he already has 'all things' through the Father (v 3). The status configuration is not reversed: it is in and through this act of humility that Jesus embodies the character and identity of God (see vs 4,5; John 1:1,2,14). It points towards his shame and glory on the cross.

Jesus washing the disciples' feet is both an extraordinary example of how they should treat each other and an expression of how he loves them: completely and fully to the end of his life (v 1).

'I have set you an example that you should do as I have done for you.'

**John 13:15**

## RESPOND
What would it mean for you to receive the humble love of Jesus? What would it mean for you to offer this kind of love to those around you?

. . . . . . . . . . . . . . . . . . . . . . . . . . . . . . . . . . . . . . . . . . . . . . . . .

**Bible in a year:** Jeremiah 40,41; John 15

# In the dark

## PREPARE
Stay still and quiet, being attentive to what rises to the surface of your mind, then bring that to God.

∙∙∙∙∙∙∙∙∙∙∙∙∙∙∙∙∙∙∙∙∙∙∙∙∙∙∙∙∙∙∙∙∙∙∙∙∙∙∙∙∙∙∙∙∙∙∙∙∙∙∙∙∙∙∙∙∙∙∙∙∙∙∙∙∙∙∙∙∙∙∙∙

## READ
**John 13:18–30**

## EXPLORE
My first question when reading this passage was: Why would Jesus choose as one of his disciples someone who would turn against him? The answer given is: to fulfil scripture and point to Jesus as the promised King (v 18; see Psalm 41:9). John continues to emphasise the importance of prophecy in confirming and understanding Jesus' identity. Jesus looks both backwards to the psalms and forwards to the time of his betrayal (v 19).

My second question was: Why does Jesus say who is going to betray him? Why is there a quiet conversation between Jesus and a specific disciple (vs 24,25)? It surprised me that Jesus gives a direct answer as it almost sounds like gossip (v 26)! One interpretation is that this disciple functions as a literary device used by John to emphasise that Jesus knew who would betray him, as the disciples don't seem to have heard his answer (v 28).

The nuances of the relationships between the disciples (eg vs 22,24) collide puzzlingly around the table: intimacy with Jesus is juxtaposed with Judas' furtive actions as the 'accuser' (v 27). And yet, even with his own inner turmoil (v 21), Jesus knows the secrets of their hearts and is shepherding them through the unfolding events.

> After he had said this, Jesus was troubled in spirit and testified, 'Very truly I tell you, one of you is going to betray me.'
>
> **John 13:21**

### RESPOND
Bring to God any tension or confusion you might feel between the intimacy and betrayal shown in this passage.

∙∙∙∙∙∙∙∙∙∙∙∙∙∙∙∙∙∙∙∙∙∙∙∙∙∙∙∙∙∙∙∙∙∙∙∙∙∙∙∙∙∙∙∙∙∙∙∙∙∙∙∙∙∙∙∙∙∙∙∙∙∙∙∙∙∙∙∙∙∙∙∙

**Bible in a year:** Jeremiah 42,43;  John 16

# Friday 25 October

## John 13:31–38

# Farewell, dear friends

## PREPARE

Think of a time when you said goodbye to someone you loved. What was said? How did it feel?

......................................................................................................

## READ

**John 13:31–38**

## EXPLORE

*Now. It's happening now*, Jesus is saying. *This is what it looks like for the Son of Man to be glorified...* Time is running out. Judas is on his way to the soldiers (see 18:3). And so, Jesus draws the disciples closer to him, deeper into an understanding of his identity and mission, his heart and mind. He will later offer comfort (14:1,16), but here the themes of love and glory fuse together (vs 31,32,34,35; see 12:23; 13:14) in this 'new command' (v 34). When he is no longer on the earth, the disciples' love will point to Jesus (v 35).

Chapters 14–16 are known as the 'farewell discourses' (see also Genesis 49; Deuteronomy 33). Jesus' farewell is framed with compassion for his disciples: 'little children' or 'my children' (v 33). The unusual language here, not used again in John's Gospel, reminds us instead of 1 John (eg 2:12), and places Jesus as the Father at the head of the table.

*We haven't got long. Lean in. Listen. Take these words and hold on to them, because you'll need them later, when everything feels even more dark and confusing. You'll need each other. You'll need to keep loving.*

'My children, I will be with you only a little longer. You will look for me, and just as I told the Jews, so I tell you now: where I am going, you cannot come.'

**John 13:33**

## RESPOND

Pray: 'Loving Jesus, help me to lean in and hear your words. I want to know your voice and listen to what is on your heart.'

......................................................................................................

**Bible in a year:** Jeremiah 44–46;  Psalm 119:49–72

# The Father and the Son

## PREPARE

'Praise the LORD, my soul; all my inmost being, praise his holy name' (Psalm 103:1). Use this psalm or your own choice of song to worship God.

· · · · · · · · · · · · · · · · · · · · · · · · · · · · · · · · · · · · · · · · · · ·

## READ

**John 14:1–14**

## EXPLORE

It's clear that the disciples want to stay with Jesus, but they don't really know how, or what that even means: their confusion and honesty persist. Thomas (v 5) adds to Peter's desperate questioning from the previous passage (13:36) and Philip just doesn't seem to have heard what Jesus has said (vs 7,8). What tone do you think Jesus uses in response (v 9)? Despite the gravity of his situation, Jesus still offers them comfort (v 1), which perhaps Peter especially needed to hear at this point.

So where is Jesus going? He seems sure enough that the disciples already know (v 4). The clearest answer within the passage seems to be: to the Father (v 12). Jesus circles towards this by reasserting the relationship between the Father and the Son (v 9). What themes in verses 9–14 have we already seen in our previous passages? What new ideas are brought in?

The significant events of Jesus' glorification continue to play out (v 7). Even if they don't grasp the full meaning, the disciples are on the inside of the story, witnessing the eternal mystery of the Father and the Son.

Jesus answered: 'Don't you know me, Philip, even after I have been among you such a long time? Anyone who has seen me has seen the Father ...'
**John 14:9**

## RESPOND

Pray: 'Jesus, I want to follow you, but I wasn't there with the disciples when you were explaining who you are. What does it mean for me today that you are the way, the truth and the life?'

· · · · · · · · · · · · · · · · · · · · · · · · · · · · · · · · · · · · · · · · · · ·

**Bible in a year:** Jeremiah 47,48;  John 17

# Sunday 27 October
## Psalm 10

# When God feels far away

## PREPARE
**What questions have you asked of God lately?**

....................................................................................................................

## READ
**Psalm 10**

## EXPLORE

This psalm pairs with Psalm 9 to respond to the question: What does faith in God look like in times of trouble? What emotions are expressed in the opening plea (v 1)?

Using verses 2–11, make a list of what the 'wicked man' is like (on paper if that helps). Here's my list: hunts the weak and innocent; boasts; ignores God; is prosperous; is arrogant; lies and threatens; assumes God doesn't care. I wonder if we ever get too familiar with situations like these, in ourselves or in our communities or around the world. Maybe we feel utterly powerless to bring about change and justice in the face of terror and tragedy.

In comparison and contrast, we see what God is like. You could make a second list. Verses 14–18 affirm that God sees, considers and will help those in need (v 14). He encourages, listens and defends (v 18). He is the 'King for ever and ever' (v 16).

Yet, in verse 12, there is still a cry for God to act on behalf of the helpless as if he is doing nothing. The whole psalm is framed with 'why' and the feeling that God is absent (v 1). This prayer is simultaneously a desperate plea for God to act and a reminder that he does (v 14).

> But you, God, see the trouble of the afflicted; you consider their grief and take it in hand. The victims commit themselves to you; you are the helper of the fatherless.

**Psalm 10:14**

### RESPOND
Consider today's news headlines. Pray for the Spirit's insight into those situations you find most challenging to read.

....................................................................................................................

**Bible in a year:** Jeremiah 49,50;  John 18

# Comforter

## PREPARE
Bring your body to a place of stillness before God, breathing deeply in and out.

. . . . . . . . . . . . . . . . . . . . . . . . . . . . . . . . . . . . . . . . . . . . . . . . . . . . . .

## READ
**John 14:15–31**

## EXPLORE
As the disciples struggle to pin down where Jesus is going and how they will cope, he comforts them with the promise of the Holy Spirit (v 16). Jesus explains how the 'Spirit of truth' (v 17) is part of the relationship between the Father and the Son: together, they are offering life (v 19), love, presence (v 23) and peace (v 27). Verse 27 is well-known: how does reading it in the context of Jesus' farewell discourse and promise of the Holy Spirit enrich your understanding?

What will this 'Advocate' – who already lives with them (v 17) – do? Jesus promises that the Holy Spirit will: remind the disciples of Jesus' teaching; teach them all things; be sent by the Father in Jesus' name (v 26); help them; be in them (v 17); and be with them for ever (v 16). Wow! How do these words speak to you and the Christian community you are part of?

Alongside this fledgling but powerful theology, John still keeps us aware of the advancing drama and the characters involved (v 22). At the close of the passage, Jesus is both protagonist and director – 'Come now; let us leave' (v 31) – in a simple statement of both authority and vulnerability.

> 'But the Advocate, the Holy Spirit, whom the Father will send in my name, will teach you all things and will remind you of everything I have said to you.'
>
> **John 14:26**

## RESPOND
Have you ever felt that Jesus is far away from you? Respond to the invitation that the Holy Spirit, the Comforter, is offering you today.

. . . . . . . . . . . . . . . . . . . . . . . . . . . . . . . . . . . . . . . . . . . . . . . . . . . . . .

**Bible in a year:** Jeremiah 51,52; Psalm 119:73–96

# Tuesday 29 October
## John 15:1–25

# Stay connected

## PREPARE
Take as much time as you can to look carefully at a tree or plant, noticing how the branches or leaves attach to the trunk or stalk. You could go outside, look out of a window or find a house plant.

.........................................................

## READ
**John 15:1–25**

## EXPLORE
'Vine' and 'vineyard' are used to describe and represent Israel in the Old Testament (eg Psalm 80). Jesus is a new revelation and fulfilment of this image: the 'true vine' (v 1). This organic picture, both metaphor and symbol, helps me understand what it means to 'remain in' Jesus (see also 14:23). To 'abide' means to stay attached so you can keep growing and bear fruit. Jesus is the source of life-giving love.

Although Jesus is speaking to his disciples, the words are for us too (see 17:20–26). Jesus is God abiding with us; we are entering into their eternal relationship. We will join with Jesus to bring glory to God as we bring requests in prayer (v 16). Loving one another is both his command (vs 10,12,17) and the result of being loved by him (vs 9,12), but isn't a guarantee of being loved by the world (v 18).

*There will be people and systems that oppose you. Remain in my love: keep receiving my love; keep listening to me and communicating with me; be obedient to my words; keep loving each other; stay loyal and faithful; keep me as your source of life.*

'This is to my Father's glory, that you bear much fruit, showing yourselves to be my disciples.'
**John 15:8**

## RESPOND
To help you visualise what 'fruit' looks like, read Galatians 5:22–25. How do these verses speak into your life?

.........................................................

**Bible in a year:** Lamentations 1,2; John 19

# Prepare your hearts

## PREPARE
How do you feel about the future? Are you a planner, looking ahead and writing in details in your diary, or do you prefer to go with the flow?

• • • • • • • • • • • • • • • • • • • • • • • • • • • • • • • • • • • • • • • • • •

## READ
**John 15:26 – 16:15**

## EXPLORE
The disciples had the profoundly unique privilege and responsibility of being those who walked with Jesus during his time of ministry on earth. Now, as he prepares for his death and glory, Jesus is calling them to be his witnesses (15:27), in partnership with the Spirit. We are all called to be witnesses to Jesus and his work in our lives, but as eyewitnesses and friends of the incarnated Jesus, the disciples were given a particular commission: to be the first ones, paving the way for others.

But why is Jesus telling them about the adversity that will come (16:1,4)? The disciples can hardly bear to look beyond the moment they are in (16:5). They are 'filled with grief' (16:6) – how can they possibly go on without him? What would it even mean to follow Jesus if they could no longer see him or walk with him? What comfort does Jesus offer (16:7,13)? How does this apply to you and to the church, 2,000 years after Jesus spoke these words and the text of John was written?

Jesus can see that the disciples are at their limits (16:12), but he needs to prepare their hearts (see also 13:19; 14:29; 15:11; 16:4) because of what is coming: both suffering and glory.

'All this I have told you so that you will not fall away.'

**John 16:1**

## RESPOND
Bring any particular upcoming challenges to God, reminding yourself of his presence with you.

• • • • • • • • • • • • • • • • • • • • • • • • • • • • • • • • • • • • • • • • • •

**Bible in a year:** Lamentations 3–5;  John 20

# Thursday 31 October
John 16:16–33

# Friends reunited

## PREPARE
How would you greet a dear friend or close family member that you haven't seen for a long time?

........................................................

## READ
John 16:16–33

## EXPLORE
Jesus' words to his disciples in chapters 14–16 are focused and intense. It's almost as if a cosmic spotlight is shining through time and space and the rest of history is waiting in the surrounding shadow. The disciples are holding their breath, wondering, whispering, questioning (vs 17,18). We are watching them witnessing something unprecedented, agonising, divine.

They have yet to see the crucifixion, meet Jesus after his resurrection and experience Pentecost. At this point, his death makes no sense to them. Even though they seem to come to a point of clarity and realisation about who Jesus is (vs 29,30), they need these powerful promises: the assurance of a truly glorious reunion (v 22), and that the Father will respond to their prayers (v 24).

However, even with the knowledge that they will be reunited with their dear friend (v 22), they also face the painful shock that they will all desert him (v 32). But Jesus' loving logic is that knowing these things in advance means they can still have peace in him (v 33). Their grief will make the way possible for unshakeable joy (v 22).

'So with you: now is your time of grief, but I will see you again and you will rejoice, and no one will take away your joy.'
**John 16:22**

## RESPOND
'… Jesus came and stood among them and said, "Peace be with you!" After he said this, he showed them his hands and side. The disciples were overjoyed when they saw the Lord' (John 20:19,20). Where are you finding joy today?

........................................................

**Bible in a year:** Ezekiel 1;  John 21

# Sent

## PREPARE

We have been reading how the preliminary events of Jesus' passion and glorification play out through the disciples' eyes. Has this affected how you look back upon the familiar narratives and tenets of the Christian faith?

. . . . . . . . . . . . . . . . . . . . . . . . . . . . . . . . . . . . . . . . . . . . . . . . . . . . . . . . . . . . . . . . .

## READ

**John 17:1–19**

## EXPLORE

After speaking at length to his disciples, Jesus now shifts his gaze to heaven. We see the necessity and power of prayer within the context of his close relationship with the Father. He turns to the Father to reaffirm his own mission and to declare that his hour has come: now is the time; here is the glory (v 1; see 12:23). Jesus also reaffirms why he came: to give eternal life. How does he define this (v 3)? How does this echo why the text of John's Gospel has been written (see 20:31)? We are being invited to believe and have life in his name!

The disciples are being sent into the world in the same way that Jesus was sent by the Father (v 18). And so, in addition to the preparation Jesus has given his disciples in person, in this prayer he now asks the Father for their protection and for unity. Once Jesus has gone, they will be learning how to be a community of believers persevering through troubled times and will need the 'full measure of my joy within them' (v 13; see 15:11).

'Now this is eternal life: that they know you, the only true God, and Jesus Christ, whom you have sent.'

**John 17:3**

---

## RESPOND

Remind yourself how John's Gospel starts: 'In the beginning was the Word, and the Word was with God, and the Word was God. He was with God in the beginning' (John 1:1,2).

---

. . . . . . . . . . . . . . . . . . . . . . . . . . . . . . . . . . . . . . . . . . . . . . . . . . . . . . . . . . . . . . . . .

**Bible in a year:** Ezekiel 2,3;  Psalm 119:97–120

## Saturday 2 November
John 17:20–26

# In the glory story

### PREPARE
**Bring to mind people from different churches, perhaps around the world, that you have visited or where you have friends. How do they reflect God's glory where they are?**

### READ
**John 17:20–26**

### EXPLORE
We end our reading of this pastoral yet deeply theological text where we began: with glory. There seems to be a mysterious relationship between unity and glory: we are given Jesus' glory to bring about unity, so that the world will know him (vs 22,23).

Jesus has given us his glory (v 22), and yet he prays for us to see it (v 24). If this part of Jesus' prayer is summarised as a prayer for all believers (v 20), how then do we apply Jesus' words directly to us? How do these words remain relevant when I'm having a coffee in a sunlit park, or watching the rugby, or washing up? How do I participate in glory when I am rocked by a wave of grief, or fall asleep exhausted, or go to a party, or do something I regret…?

We have been looking backwards, seeing how Jesus prepared the disciples for his death. Now, as witnesses ourselves, we look ahead. We are brought into the story and into his love (v 26). There is even more waiting for us when we see Jesus as he is, in all the fullness of glory and love and life that has been there from the beginning.

> 'Father, I want those you have given me to be with me where I am, and to see my glory, the glory you have given me because you loved me before the creation of the world.'
>
> **John 17:24**

### RESPOND
In what different ways do you pray? You could write your own prayer based on one of the themes we have seen in John's Gospel.

**Bible in a year:** Ezekiel 4,5; James 1

# When doubt comes to call

## PREPARE

**What injustices in the world, or in your local community, do you feel most strongly about? How is God using you or others to bring justice and peace?**

. . . . . . . . . . . . . . . . . . . . . . . . . . . . . . . . . . . . . . . . . . . . . . . . . . . . . . . . . . . . . . . . . . . . . . . . . . . . . . . . . . . . . . . . . . . . .

## READ

**Psalm 11**

## EXPLORE

This psalm opens with a clear statement of trust. It is a rebuke to the cynical voice which points to a way out (v 1) and draws attention to powerlessness in the face of imminent danger (vs 2,3). Extending this voice of trust in verses 4–7, the psalmist explains why he still chooses to turn to God, despite his terrifying situation: God is on his throne, sees all things, hates violence, will punish those who are wicked, is righteous, loves justice and will reveal himself to the upright.

Looking back over ancient and recent history, the death, fear and pain caused by local and international conflict don't go away. When I listened to the news on the radio this morning, I cried with anger, sorrow and helplessness. Is God passive and emotionless when people get hurt? Why doesn't he step in and stop wars? Why would he hate and punish people?

We have a choice: to turn to our own anger, cynicism and finite ability to effect change, or to join the psalmist (vs 4–7) by trusting in God's justice and goodness. Instead of being passive, trusting God becomes active – an action we take to lead us forwards.

For the LORD is righteous, he loves justice; the upright will see his face.

**Psalm 11:7**

## RESPOND

Do you feel able to be a voice of hope and faith rather than despair and doubt? Who could you speak words of life and encouragement to this week?

. . . . . . . . . . . . . . . . . . . . . . . . . . . . . . . . . . . . . . . . . . . . . . . . . . . . . . . . . . . . . . . . . . . . . . . . . . . . . . . . . . . . . . . . . . . . .

**Bible in a year:** Ezekiel 6,7;  James 2

# Flawed leaders and a redemptive God

The stories in 1 and 2 Samuel take place just over 1,000 years before Jesus' birth. They straddle the time between the Exodus of the people out of Egypt under Moses' leadership (1200 BC) and the anointing of the first kings in Israel, Saul and David.

About the writer
**David Bruce**

David is a retired Presbyterian minister, living near Belfast in Northern Ireland. He is married to Zoe, and they are proud parents, and now also, grandparents. In the past, David was Director of SU in Northern Ireland, and also Regional Director for Britain and Ireland.

These were times of great spiritual confusion – the book of Judges records that 'In those days Israel had no king; everyone did as they saw fit' (21:25). The pressure to identify and anoint kings was great, and so it came to be, even if this was understood to be God's second best.

In the chapters in this series, Saul is identified as the first king. Despite starting well, however, he quickly loses the plot and is set aside for a new kingly line in David, the youngest son of Jesse. The themes emerging are about leadership, character and the kingly rule of God. We will see examples of dreadful foolishness in leadership and stories of faith-filled boldness. We will also be led repeatedly to see how God takes the things that are not, and uses them to his glory. This includes the flawed leaders we will see in these pages, just as it points to the kingdom which Jesus would teach about and establish, where the last shall be first (Matthew 19:30) and the tiny mustard seed will become a generous home for the birds of the air (Luke 13:18,19).

# Foolish leadership

## PREPARE
Think of the turbulent years before these events. The sorry story of Eli and his corrupt sons (1 Samuel 4) led to their descendant being named Ichabod: 'the glory has departed'. Would God still bless his people?

. . . . . . . . . . . . . . . . . . . . . . . . . . . . . . . . . . . . . . . . . . . . . . . . . . . . . . . . . . . . . . . . . . .

## READ
**1 Samuel 13:1–15**

## EXPLORE
In Samuel the prophet's eyes, Saul was trouble. True, Saul had been anointed as king, and was therefore accorded due respect for his office. But the very idea of kingship was, in Samuel's eyes, God's second-best plan for the people (1 Samuel 12:12,17). Today's reading confirms this, showing that Saul had much to learn. With his son Jonathan, he set up a confrontation with the old enemy, the Philistines, at Gilgal (vs 3–6). A foolish mistake. Rather than wait for God's blessing in the person of Samuel, he sought to act alone – even to take Samuel's place as priest. A foolish over-reach.

When believers say or sing that 'Jesus is Lord', there needs to be clear evidence in their lives, or their words are hollow. See how Saul raced ahead of God and sowed the seeds of much more conflict in years to come. He didn't wait for God's blessing, but tried to make it happen on his own terms (vs 8–10). He sought to justify his actions, rather than acknowledging his foolish sin (vs 11,12).

'What have you done?' asked Samuel ... 'You have done a foolish thing'.
**1 Samuel 13:11,13**

## RESPOND
As you learn from Saul's poor decision-making, think of ways in which you can make God the centre of your own, so that Jesus truly is Lord in your life today.

. . . . . . . . . . . . . . . . . . . . . . . . . . . . . . . . . . . . . . . . . . . . . . . . . . . . . . . . . . . . . . . . . . .

**Bible in a year:** Ezekiel 8,9;  Psalm 119:121–144

# Tuesday 5 November

1 Samuel 15:1–31

# Tough leadership

## PREPARE

**In reading this brutal story today, try to see beyond the awfulness of violence to the determination of God that we be 'ransomed, healed, restored, forgiven' (Henry Lyte, 'Praise My Soul', 1834).**

· · · · · · · · · · · · · · · · · · · · · · · · · · · · · · · · · · · · · · · · · · · · · · · · · · · · · · · · · · · · ·

## READ

**1 Samuel 15:1–31**

## EXPLORE

The Amalekites had a long history of hate-filled, genocidal opposition to the Hebrew people (Exodus 17; Deuteronomy 25). There are things in human history which are so desperately evil that God will not be diverted from acting against them. Such were the Amalekites and their campaign of annihilation. God's instruction that they and their possessions be attacked and destroyed was harsh but abundantly clear (vs 2,3). Even so, Saul failed in his anointed mission. He spared the Amalekite king and kept the battle plunder (vs 7–9).

Sin is a desperate condition that affects everyone: its wages is death (Romans 6:23). God's implacable determination to remove the sin-filled Amalekites, who were determined to kill his people, points to another deep sacrifice of life in the future. It shows God's unshakeable commitment to removing the sin that kills us, by sending Jesus to die in our place. Had God pulled back from the desolation of the cross, we would still be 'dead in [our] transgressions and sins' (Ephesians 2:1). But he pressed on to the place where new life was offered to the world.

> But Samuel replied: 'Does the LORD delight in burnt offerings and sacrifices as much as in obeying the LORD? To obey is better than sacrifice ...'
>
> **1 Samuel 15:22**

## RESPOND

Thank God for the cross today, while with sadness lamenting the reality of sin, confessing your own sin as necessary today.

· · · · · · · · · · · · · · · · · · · · · · · · · · · · · · · · · · · · · · · · · · · · · · · · · · · · · · · · · · · · ·

**Bible in a year:** Ezekiel 10,11;  James 3

# Unlikely leadership

## PREPARE

'Not by might nor by power, but by my Spirit, says the Lᴏʀᴅ Almighty' (Zechariah 4:6). How do you experience this?

## READ

**1 Samuel 16:1–13**

## EXPLORE

Saul's son Jonathan might well have expected to become king, continuing his father's line, but God would not have it. So many were Saul's failings that another line would be started, a line which would extend forward in time to Jesus.

The choice of Jesse's youngest son as heir apparent points to how God rules as King of kings. He subverts all our expectations of greatness and power. Saul started well in this respect – a member of the lowliest clan in the smallest tribe of Benjamin (1 Samuel 9:21). His character flaws, however, showed that he would never grow up. David was a boy among men, yet he was the one God chose, and while he had many flaws he remained faithful in a way that Saul did not.

God takes the long view, seeing the end from the beginning. In his kingdom, unlikely things happen. A tiny mustard seed becomes a huge tree, providing a place for many birds to perch (Luke 13:18,19). A farmer sowing seed produces a massive crop (Matthew 13:8). A fisherman's nets bulge to the point of bursting (John 21:6). The first are last and the last are first (Matthew 19:30).

So he sent for him and had him brought in. He was glowing with health and had a fine appearance and handsome features. Then the Lᴏʀᴅ said, 'Rise and anoint him; this is the one.'

**1 Samuel 16:12**

## RESPOND

Thank God today that God's rule in the world is not like ours. Take time to pray for legislators in your own country, that they would model their leadership on Jesus' example.

**Bible in a year:** Ezekiel 12,13;  James 4

## Thursday 7 November
1 Samuel 17:1–27

# Faith-filled leadership

## PREPARE
**If you are facing a stubborn problem without a human solution, draw comfort and challenge from David, who saw the Lord at work where others thought he had deserted them.**

## READ
**1 Samuel 17:1–27**

## EXPLORE
Six weeks of relentless taunting by the Philistine champion warrior Goliath left the Israelite army paralysed with fear (vs 11,16). Notice that neither Goliath's aggressive, confident words of defiance (vs 8–10) nor the Israelites' fearful responses to his words (v 25) made any reference to the Lord. An unbeliever cannot be expected to factor God into their thinking, but the Israelite army had no such excuse. See how easily fear can remove all thoughts of God from us.

The opposite of fear is neither bravery nor courage – although both are necessary in military conflict. The deepest antidote to fear is faith. When the young David witnessed this stand-off, his response was entirely different from that of the soldiers (v 26). David shows that Goliath's blustering defiance is a much more serious matter than just the boasting of a bully. Goliath was recklessly defying the living God, which ultimately places him on the losing side. David's words are infused with faith, a gift of God which flowed from his anointing by the Spirit (1 Samuel 16:13; Ephesians 2:8,9).

'Who is this uncircumcised Philistine that he should defy the armies of the living God?'
**1 Samuel 17:26b**

### RESPOND
'Who is on the Lord's side? Who will serve the King?' (Frances R Havergal, 1877). Reflect on the blessing of faithful trust in the Lord.

**Bible in a year:** Ezekiel 14,15;  James 5

# Talented leadership

## PREPARE
God's ways are not our ways. Swords and spears might have been the obvious solution to the Goliath problem, but God had another plan. Allow yourself to be surprised by God's ways.

## READ
**1 Samuel 17:28–58**

## EXPLORE
Once again, we see God's delight in the small, apparently insignificant, being lifted up. So much so that David and Goliath are even now a metaphor for the unlikely victory of the underdog.

Hidden in plain sight in this story is what set David apart from everyone else on the battlefield that day. David's attempts to persuade King Saul that he should be the one to take on Goliath hinge on his worldview. His talents were part of the process – he killed a lion and a bear, so he had the skills. But this was not enough, even with Saul's heavy armour on his back. David repeated what he had said to others: Goliath's days are numbered because he 'has defied the armies of the living God' (v 36). It was surely this testimony of faith which convinced Saul to allow him to represent the people: 'Go, and the Lord be with you' (v 37).

The simplicity of the manner of his victory – a sling and a stone – was the most powerful indicator that God went before him on to the field. David knew that God had equipped him through natural talents and spiritual vision to serve him.

> 'All those gathered here will know that it is not by sword or spear that the Lord saves; for the battle is the Lord's, and he will give all of you into our hands.'
>
> **1 Samuel 17:47**

## RESPOND
What are you good at? Ask yourself how this talent is being used in the service of Christ. Is there a new opportunity for service before you?

**Bible in a year:** Ezekiel 16,17; Psalm 119:145–176

## Saturday 9 November
1 Samuel 18:1–16

# Servant leadership

## PREPARE
Transitions in leadership can be fragile moments, for churches and nations alike. As you read today be conscious of fragile states around the world, and of those who suffer through regime change.

. . . . . . . . . . . . . . . . . . . . . . . . . . . . . . . . . . . . . . . . . . . . . . . . . . . . . . . . . . . . .

## READ
**1 Samuel 18:1–16**

## EXPLORE
The warmth of the friendship between Jonathan and David contrasts deeply with King Saul's growing suspicion and hatred of his successor. Jonathan might be the expected heir, but David will be king, and Jonathan both knows and gladly accepts this. By giving David his symbols of status and strength (v 4) Jonathan was publicly offering him his loyalty. Meanwhile, Saul's jealousy of David's growing popularity among the people sours to become paranoia (v 9).

The finest leaders are those who do not aspire to it. Enduring leaders are those who do not hold on to power beyond their time. Such people who have overstayed their welcome are usually pushed out – and this was Saul's experience. God himself was loosening Saul's grip on power (v 10).

As history would show, David was by no means perfect and repeated many of Saul's mistakes. Kingship was the people's ambition, rather than God's best for them, and they paid the price of flawed human leadership. Their faulty kings would, centuries later, lead them into exile in Babylon. God might have said, 'I told you so'.

In everything he did he had great success, because the LORD was with him.

**1 Samuel 18:14**

## RESPOND
Think of a Christian leader whom you can affirm today. Send them an encouraging message. Let them know that you are praying for them and then spend time doing it.

. . . . . . . . . . . . . . . . . . . . . . . . . . . . . . . . . . . . . . . . . . . . . . . . . . . . . . . . . . . . .

**Bible in a year:** Ezekiel 18,19;  1 Peter 1

# Words matter

## PREPARE
Thank God that his Word is truth, and that you hold it in your hands or view it on a screen today. Pray: 'Lord, open my eyes that I may see wonderful things in your word today.'

## READ
**Psalm 12**

## EXPLORE
'Vile things' are honoured by the human race (v 8). When we become used to this, such that we tolerate it without comment, we show that our inner selves have been damaged. The source of the damage is words. Lies, flattering, deception (v 2), boasting (v 3), bullying (v 4) or malign slandering (v 5): words matter, to the extent that what is written and spoken can shape, reshape and even overthrow an entire culture. James insists that human beings cannot tame the human tongue (James 3:8). It is like a spark which sets off a wild fire.

Scripture is different. These 66 books, full of words, tutor us towards the flawless, precious purity of God's voice (v 6). He speaks truth (John 17:17), which has an effect, pushing back the corruption of language which rots and destroys the human spirit. Truth is important, because it bursts the bubble of the arrogant who 'freely strut about' (v 8). It slows and then halts the progress of falsehood in its tracks, offering the world both safety and protection (v 7).

> And the words of the LORD are flawless, like silver purified in a crucible, like gold refined seven times.
>
> **Psalm 12:6**

## RESPOND
Give thanks for the work of Scripture Union and the Bible societies which make God's Word available and understandable to millions of people throughout the world. Pray for truth to be honoured in all cultures.

**Bible in a year:** Ezekiel 20,21; 1 Peter 2

# Spotlight on...

# The Bible and me –
## a writer's experience of the Bible

In these Spotlight articles we ask *Daily Bread* writers to tell us a little about what the Bible means to them. For this issue we talked with **David Bruce**.

David Bruce is a minister in the Presbyterian Church in Ireland. He was formerly General Director of Scripture Union in Northern Ireland and has also served as a staff worker for UCCF. In 2020 he was elected as Moderator of the General Assembly of the Presbyterian Church, serving for two terms. He is now retired but remains active in preaching and teaching. He is married to Zoe and they have four adult children and two grandchildren. They live near Lisburn in Northern Ireland.

### What was your early experience of the Bible?

As a child I attended Sunday School sporadically, so became familiar with many of the major Bible stories, even if I had little understanding of how they held together or indeed what they meant. We didn't read the Bible together as a family, so I had little real exposure to its message at a personal level. It did not become real to me until I was a young adult.

### How did your appreciation of the Bible grow as you got older?

I came to personal faith in Christ when I was 18, and suddenly found the Bible to be an open rather than a closed book. The Living Bible translation had just been published, and I devoured it, as it was much more accessible than the Authorized King James Version which I had previously seen. I became aware that God the Holy Spirit was at work as I read, and that repeatedly I would sense God's leading through what I was discovering. I also began to use SU *Daily Bread* notes and got into the good habit of reading a portion of scripture each day. When the NIV was published in 1979, I bought a copy which I still have on my shelf! It remains the translation I prefer today.

At university I became involved in the Christian Union, and for the first time I took part in group Bible study with others. So gradually, as the months and then years went by, I realised that the Bible had become central to both my understanding of the Christian faith and also my view of the world. So it has continued over five decades.

**You are a minister who teaches the Bible. Did your training in theology change your approach to Scripture?**

Theological college can be a challenging place, because differing ideas about Scripture are explored openly, among believers and sceptics alike. At first, I struggled to see how this could be helpful – especially because the Bible had become more than a text to me – it was a matter of the heart as well as the head. But reflecting upon those years, I am grateful for learning something of the biblical languages, and for examining more rigorously how the Bible came to us. As a preacher and teacher, I have found the tools of biblical study learned at college to be of real worth and I'm grateful for the experience – and with this background I am better able to say with confidence that the Bible is indeed God's living Word. It is a rich tapestry of different threads – narrative, prophetic, poetic and visionary – and the weave these and

other parts create is spectacular. Knowing Scripture – its origins, stories and themes – is as important as loving Scripture as the source of personal spiritual comfort. When we know it and love it, we see more and more of the God it reveals.

**And what about now?**

I am constantly amazed to discover how God uses his Word in the lives of his people. It shapes character, builds resilience, offers guidance, establishes ethical and moral principles and points inexorably towards Jesus who is the light of the world. Whether as a husband, father and grandfather or as a church leader, I rely entirely upon its wisdom and depend daily upon its truth. I recognise that today the Bible is under critical scrutiny like never before, and is dismissed widely, even being seen as a negative influence on our culture. One of the major challenges before the church is to speak well of Scripture and be determined to hold it as central in worship and preaching. We have little to say without it, and nothing that will be of transformational help to a lost and broken world.

**David Bruce**

# Hope for troubled times

Paul wrote these letters to Thessalonians who had come to faith in Christ through his earlier ministry. From the warm tone of his letter, they clearly meant a lot to him (1 Thessalonians 2:7). He was proud of the way they grasped the gospel (1 Thessalonians 2:19,20).

## About the writer
**Ali Walton**

Ali is Associate Rector at Emmanuel Church, Loughborough. She is married to Steve. They share their home with a lovely Border Terrier called Flora. Ali enjoys reading, walking in the beautiful Leicestershire countryside and all things crafty and creative.

However, they were beginning to wobble in their faith. In both letters we see that they were facing trials, suffering, confusion and divisions.

In 1 Thessalonians Paul addresses opposition from non-Christians around them (1:6); temptation to sexual impurity (4:3,4); worry that those who died before Jesus' return would be separated from those still alive (4:13–18); and preoccupation with identifying the precise time of Jesus' return.

Paul continues to encourage and build them up in 2 Thessalonians. They continue to face persecution (chapter 1), confusion about what will happen when Jesus returns (chapter 2) and burdens caused by some who refused to work and became gossips (chapter 3).

In both letters we read Paul's emphasis on strengthening their faith (2 Thessalonians 2:15) and the certainty of Christian hope in encouraging them to keep going and growing (1 Thessalonians 5:23,24).

The similarities between the Thessalonian society and many societies in the world today are striking in terms of persecution: we see temptations in the world around us and divisions within churches. We can become discouraged just as the Thessalonians did. As we read these letters, may we too know our faith and hope being strengthened by the Lord.

# My dear Thessalonians...

## PREPARE
In today's passage Paul encourages the Thessalonians. Ask the Lord to encourage you when reading today's verses.

· · · · · · · · · · · · · · · · · · · · · · · · · · · · · · · · · · · · · · · · · · · · · · · · · · · · · · · · · ·

## READ
1 Thessalonians 1:1–10

## EXPLORE
Paul, Silas and Timothy send greetings (v 1). Paul states that the Thessalonians' identity is rooted in their relationship with God the Father and the Lord Jesus Christ. Grace and peace are also found in Jesus (see John 14:27).

In verses 2 and 3 Paul says that they give thanks for the Thessalonian Christians. What three things does Paul thank God for (v 3)? These are rooted in faith, love and hope in Christ. Faith refers to constant loyalty and trust. It takes willpower to keep trusting Jesus, especially in times of hardship. Take a moment to identify the fruit of Christ's faith, love and hope working in you.

Paul reminds them of how they came to faith in Christ (vs 4–7). Identify his reasons for knowing that God chose them (vs 4,5). He helps them to understand how precious they are to God (see Isaiah 44:1,2). They came to faith at a time of suffering (v 6). In verse 7 Paul speaks of them modelling faith to others. What was it that caused this (v 6)?

In verses 8–10 Paul reminds them that they are famous for following Jesus faithfully. Worshipping idols was common in their culture. These verses demonstrate how radically their lives have changed since they came to faith in Jesus.

We remember before our God and Father your work produced by faith, your labour prompted by love, and your endurance inspired by hope in our Lord Jesus Christ.

1 Thessalonians 1:3

## RESPOND
Thank God for bringing you to faith in Christ and that you are precious to him. Pray for strength to keep trusting in him, even in hard times.

· · · · · · · · · · · · · · · · · · · · · · · · · · · · · · · · · · · · · · · · · · · · · · · · · · · · · · · · · ·

**Bible in a year:** Ezekiel 22,23; Psalms 120–122

## Tuesday 12 November
### 1 Thessalonians 2:1–16

# With care and love

## PREPARE
**Think about the conflict, pressures and suffering that your church leaders face. Remember these as you read today's passage.**

........................................................................................

## READ
**1 Thessalonians 2:1–16**

## EXPLORE

Paul describes his ministry in Thessalonica, explaining his behaviour in defence of criticism while simultaneously encouraging the Christians. He describes his courage (vs 1,2), his integrity (vs 3–7a) and his tender care (vs 7b–12).

The courage Paul shows in sharing the gospel after persecution and suffering in Philippi is remarkable (v 2). What has given him the motivation for this (v 2)?

Verses 3–7a describe Paul's integrity demonstrated during his ministry in Thessalonica: a model of how to respond to pressure and conflict in a Christ-like way. Imagine you are facing pressure and conflict because of your faith. How would these verses encourage you?

Paul says that he, Silas and Barnabus were like young children among the Thessalonians (v 7a). Other versions use the word 'gentle'. The picture of a nursing mother (v 7b) emphasises the loving, tender, caring nature of their ministry. Identify these characteristics of Paul's ministry to the Thessalonians (verses 7–13). Looking at verses 3–13, what might their ministry have looked like if they had insisted on asserting their authority (v 6)?

In verses 13–16 Paul praises the Thessalonians for their endurance in the face of persecution. Verse 16 is a salutary warning against the persecutors. Persecuting Christians comes with serious health warnings.

## ... we were delighted to share with you not only the gospel of God but our lives as well.
**1 Thessalonians 2:7,8**

---

### RESPOND
Pray for church leaders to have courage, integrity and tender care in their ministries, especially in times of pressure, conflict and suffering.

---

........................................................................................

**Bible in a year:** Ezekiel 24,25; 1 Peter 3

# I'm longing to see you

## PREPARE
Pray that as you read today's passage you will see how the Lord provides encouragement for those who need it.

.........................................................................

## READ
**1 Thessalonians 2:17 – 3:5**

## EXPLORE
There is an intimacy about Paul's longing to see the Thessalonians. The proverb 'out of sight, out of mind' did not apply to Paul and the Thessalonians.

Verses 17 and 18 describe Paul's longing to see them. He felt their separation keenly – like children being torn from parents and being orphaned. He made every effort to see them, but Satan blocked his way (v 18). It is not clear what Paul meant by this. He may have been referring to an illness or to persecution and opposition.

We see in verses 19 and 20 Paul's pride in the Thessalonians as a proud parent boasts of the achievements of their children. Notice how extravagantly he describes the Thessalonians. Look back to 1:3 for the reasons for Paul's pride. Paul saw those who came to faith in Christ through him as the fruit of his life and ministry in Christ (see 2 Corinthians 1:14).

In 3:1–5 point to the depth of Paul's love for the Thessalonians as he prioritises their needs above his own. What caused Paul's fear for them (v 5)? His concern was so great that he sent Timothy to them, despite his own desire for Timothy's company (vs 1,2). Reading verses 2 and 3, what was Paul's purpose in sending Timothy?

We sent Timothy, who is our brother and co-worker in God's service in spreading the gospel of Christ, to strengthen and encourage you in your faith

**1 Thessalonians 3:2**

---

## RESPOND
Think of the people who encourage you. Thank the Lord for them. Pray that you might be an encouragement to others.

---

.........................................................................

**Bible in a year:** Ezekiel 26,27; 1 Peter 4

## Thursday 14 November
### 1 Thessalonians 3:6–13

# Good news from Timothy

## PREPARE

Today's reading is about good news. The good news of Jesus is the best news of all. Thank the Lord for all he has done for you.

••••••••••••••••••••••••••••••••••••••••••••••••••

## READ

**1 Thessalonians 3:6–13**

## EXPLORE

Timothy brought Paul good news. The Thessalonians continued to grow in faith and love (v 6). Paul took the good news of Jesus to the Thessalonians. Now Timothy's report is good news for Paul. The longing to see each other was obviously mutual (v 6). No doubt the encouragement was mutual too (v 7).

Verse 8 conveys the importance the Thessalonians' ongoing faith had for Paul. Put yourself in his shoes. What did he mean by this? He was revitalised by knowing that the Thessalonians were standing firm despite tough tests. Verse 9 shows how much this meant to Paul. He asks how he can give thanks for all the joy he has received because of them. Look at verse 10 to discover how he answers his own question.

In verses 11–13 Paul prays three things for the Thessalonians. Identify what those three things are. In verse 12 Paul indicated that it is only the Lord Jesus who can help Christians to love each other. They were not to lose sight of that, however hard the pressure became. We see the third thing Paul prayed in verse 13. His focus is on the state of their lives when Jesus returns.

May he strengthen your hearts so that you will be blameless and holy in the presence of our God and Father when our Lord Jesus comes with all his holy ones.

**1 Thessalonians 3:13**

## RESPOND

In the light of Paul's prayer, how can we pray for ourselves in our own walk with Jesus? Take a few moments to think about that before you pray.

••••••••••••••••••••••••••••••••••••••••••••••••••

**Bible in a year:** Ezekiel 28,29; 1 Peter 5

# Love God; love each other

## PREPARE
Today's passage challenges us to be holy. Ask the Lord to show you areas of your life where you need help with holiness.

. . . . . . . . . . . . . . . . . . . . . . . . . . . . . . . . . . . . . . . . . . . . . . . . . . . . . . . . . . . . . . . . . . . . . . . . .

## READ
**1 Thessalonians 4:1–12**

## EXPLORE
Paul turns to challenging the Thessalonians to lead holy lives.

Verses 1 and 2 remind them that Paul has shared the good news of Jesus with them and instructed them in how to live to please God. These instructions carry the full authority of the Lord (v 2). Knowing the Lord Jesus means living in new ways, being close to God and serving him wholeheartedly.

Paul describes what being made holy (vs 3–6) involves. What things are incompatible with this? Summarise what Paul says about the sort of lives we should live (v 7). The Thessalonians had to learn self-control over their bodies because they were temples of the Holy Spirit (1 Corinthians 6:19,20). Identify areas where God wants to make you holy. Paul completes this section with a warning about the serious consequences of failing to be holy (v 8).

Verses 9–12 link loving each other (as brother and sister, v 10) with leading a quiet life (v 11). Why is it important to make this link? Paul recognises that the Thessalonians love each other, but encourages them to do so even more. The call to be holy, faithful and full of integrity should be expressed in the details of everyday life. Why does Paul say this (v 12)?

For God did not call us to be impure, but to live a holy life.

**1 Thessalonians 4:7**

## RESPOND
Confess to the Lord ways you are failing to be holy. Ask him to forgive you and give you strength to be more like him.

. . . . . . . . . . . . . . . . . . . . . . . . . . . . . . . . . . . . . . . . . . . . . . . . . . . . . . . . . . . . . . . . . . . . . . . . .

**Bible in a year:** Ezekiel 30,31; Psalms 123–125

# Saturday 16 November
## 1 Thessalonians 4:13–18

# Encourage each other

## PREPARE
Ask yourself what difference it makes for a Christian to have hope in death because of Jesus' death, resurrection and future return.

. . . . . . . . . . . . . . . . . . . . . . . . . . . . . . . . . . . . . . . . . . . . . . . . . . . . . . . . . . .

## READ
**1 Thessalonians 4:13–18**

## EXPLORE
Paul teaches the Thessalonians about Christian hope in the face of death. Their cultural background believed that there was nothing beyond death, and so people grieved with no hope. However, the situation is different for Christians, who believe that Jesus' resurrection has defeated death once and for all (v 13).

Paul describes death as 'sleep' (v 13). Why do you think he does this? Western culture is uncomfortable with death. Think of words you've heard people use instead. Rather than using 'sleep' as a way of avoiding death, Paul was following Jesus' example in referring to death as 'sleep' (see Matthew 9:24 and the story of Jairus' daughter).

Verse 15 suggests that the Thessalonians worried that those who died before Jesus came again would be separated from Jesus. Therefore, they grieved as people without hope. Paul says emphatically that Christians who have already died will be the first to rise from death when Jesus returns. How might Paul's words in verse 14 have comforted the Thessalonians? How might they comfort you?

Look at the amazing description of Jesus' return in verses 16 and 17. Paul wrote this description to encourage the Thessalonians. Think about how this description encourages you.

> For we believe that Jesus died and rose again, and so we believe that God will bring with Jesus those who have fallen asleep in him.

**1 Thessalonians 4:14**

---

### RESPOND
Thank the Lord for the hope we have as Christians (v 14). Pray for those who are grieving, that they will know Jesus' comfort and hope.

---

. . . . . . . . . . . . . . . . . . . . . . . . . . . . . . . . . . . . . . . . . . . . . . . . . . . . . . . . . . .

**Bible in a year:** Ezekiel 32,33;  2 Peter 1

# How long, Lord?

## PREPARE
**Remember a time when God felt absent. What did you do?**

## READ
**Psalm 13**

## EXPLORE
We do not know what David was facing when writing this psalm. We do know that when life is hard, we may feel that God has forgotten us. The rawness of David's emotions in this psalm encourages us. It gives us permission to express the same questions and feelings as David.

In verses 1 and 2 David cries out to God in desperation. He feels that God has forgotten him (v 1), is hiding from him (v 1) and is allowing David's enemies to triumph over him (v 2). Count how many times David asks, 'How long?' He is longing for God to rescue him. When you are waiting for God to hear you, how do you cope?

David now asks the Lord to bring him out of darkness into light so that he does not die (v 3). Next he asks God to rescue him because he does not want his enemies gloating that the Lord failed him (v 4).

David's mood in verses 5 and 6 changes completely. We don't know whether something dramatic has happened to cause this. It may be that David is encouraging himself by affirming his trust in the Lord that the day will come when he once more rejoices and sings God's praises.

But I trust in your unfailing love; my heart rejoices in your salvation.

**Psalm 13:5**

## RESPOND
Look back over this psalm. Think about how it might help you to pray when you are having a hard time. You might also pray this psalm for someone you know who is having a hard time.

**Bible in a year:** Ezekiel 34,35; 2 Peter 2

# Monday 18 November

## 1 Thessalonians 5:1–11

# Be prepared and persevere

## PREPARE

**Think about how you prepare to go on holiday. Are you ready well in advance, or do you leave everything to the last minute?**

. . . . . . . . . . . . . . . . . . . . . . . . . . . . . . . . . . . . . . . . . . . . . . . . . . . . . .

## READ

**1 Thessalonians 5:1–11**

## EXPLORE

Paul turns his attention to encouraging those who are still alive to live as if ready for Jesus to return at any moment.

First, Paul encourages them to be ready for the night thief (vs 1–3). Jesus used the same picture in Matthew 24:42–44. Look at verse 2. According to Paul, when will Jesus come again? In verse 3 Paul warns against people who make false promises about peace and security.

Secondly, Paul encourages the Thessalonians to be people of the light and the day (vs 4–7). Looking at these verses, identify the contrasts between people of the light and people of the dark. In what ways do these verses challenge you?

Thirdly, Paul encourages the Thessalonians to be ready for the battle (vs 8–11). The Thessalonians had been quarrelling about when and where Jesus would return. Paul was afraid

that they would slip back into former habits of the night and dark. Paul uses the idea of armour here in the sense of soldiers being disciplined and prepared for battle. He refers again to faith, hope and love (remember 1:3). The key to combating their fears lies in the power of these three, not in knowing the date and time of Jesus' return.

> But since we belong to the day, let us be sober, putting on faith and love as a breastplate, and the hope of salvation as a helmet.

**1 Thessalonians 5:8**

---

## RESPOND

Confess to God anything in your life that is hidden in the dark. Now ask the Lord to help you to live in readiness for him to come again.

---

. . . . . . . . . . . . . . . . . . . . . . . . . . . . . . . . . . . . . . . . . . . . . . . . . . . . . .

**Bible in a year:** Ezekiel 36,37; Psalms 126–128

# Finally and farewell

## PREPARE
Imagine you are saying farewell to dear friends. What would you say to them? What might they say to you? Ask God to speak to you today.

## READ
**1 Thessalonians 5:12–28**

## EXPLORE
In these final verses Paul instructs the Thessalonians on how to continue living the Christian life.

In verses 12–15, Paul addresses issues of their attitude to their leaders and community life. How might these instructions help a church now to avoid division, particularly in times of change?

Paul then turns to maintaining holy attitudes in the face of suffering (vs 16–22). What three holy habits does Paul tell them to cultivate and why (vs 16–18)? They are to avoid quenching the Holy Spirit by treating prophecies with contempt, and must reject every kind of evil (vs 19–22). Holding on to good (v 21) was essential for living out these holy habits.

Paul follows with a prayer for peace and holiness (vs 23,24). He knew that they might be tempted to give up under stress and suffering. How would verse 24 have encouraged them?

Finally (vs 25–28), Paul asks them to pray for him and his co-workers. He assumes that they will know what to pray for. The 'holy kiss' (v 26) was a well-established practice in the early church, symbolising the strength of their relationships with each other. Paul finishes as he began (see 1:1), with a blessing of grace.

> May God himself, the God of peace, sanctify you through and through. May your whole spirit, soul and body be kept blameless at the coming of our Lord Jesus Christ.
>
> **1 Thessalonians 5:23**

## RESPOND
Choose one of these verse sections. Pray through the verses either for yourself or for your church community.

# Wednesday 20 November

2 Thessalonians 1:1–12

# Grace and peace to you

**PREPARE**
Remember how you came to faith. Thank the Lord for helping you to grow in faith.

. . . . . . . . . . . . . . . . . . . . . . . . . . . . . . . . . . . . . . . . . . . . . . . . . . . . . . . . . . . . . . . .

**READ**
**2 Thessalonians 1:1–12**

**EXPLORE**
The opening of 2 Thessalonians is very similar to that of 1 Thessalonians. Note the importance Paul gives to God the Father and the Lord Jesus Christ. He prays for the Thessalonians to know grace and peace.

Paul gives thanks for the Thessalonians (vs 3,4). He refers to the persecutions and trials they are enduring (v 4). Look at these verses. Identify what Paul gives thanks for and what he boasts about.

Paul again writes about the second coming of Jesus (vs 5–10). His focus is on what Jesus will do. Paul encourages the Thessalonians in two ways. In the short term (v 5), they should be encouraged that God trusts them to remain faithful to him, even in trials and suffering. Long term (vs 6–10), Paul reminds them that God is just. Those who do not obey Jesus will be shut out from God's presence. Read verses 6–9 again and notice the detail of Paul's description. Verse 10 is the peak of Paul's encouragement.

Imagine how the Thessalonians would have felt when they heard verse 10.

In verses 11 and 12, Paul prays for the Thessalonians. He prays that God's power would continue to work in them so that their desire to do good, prompted by their faith, would bear fruit.

> With this in mind, we constantly pray for you, that our God may make you worthy of his calling, and that by his power he may bring to fruition your every desire for goodness and your every deed prompted by faith.

**2 Thessalonians 1:11**

---

**RESPOND**
Pray Paul's prayer for yourself, saying 'me' instead of 'you'. Now pray the passage again, for your church.

---

. . . . . . . . . . . . . . . . . . . . . . . . . . . . . . . . . . . . . . . . . . . . . . . . . . . . . . . . . . . . . . . .

**Bible in a year:** Ezekiel 40,41; 1 John 1

# No need to panic

**PREPARE**
**This passage is complex. Ask the Lord to help you to understand it.**

· · · · · · · · · · · · · · · · · · · · · · · · · · · · · · · · · · · · · · · · · ·

**READ**
**2 Thessalonians 2:1–12**

**EXPLORE**
These verses are confusing. However, Paul's purpose is to remind the Thessalonians that, despite gloomy happenings, the Lord Jesus Christ will prevail and his people be vindicated.

Paul encourages the Thessalonians to persevere and not be thrown off-balance by teaching which allegedly came from him but actually did not (vs 1,2). He tells them not to be afraid because 'the day of the Lord' has not yet come (vs 2,3).

Next, Paul refers to what will happen when 'the man of lawlessness' (v 3) comes (vs 3–10). First will be a great rebellion against God (v 4). The 'man of lawlessness' can also be called both anti-Christ and anti-Law. Paul does not explain who this person is, only that he is to come and will be a rebel in league with Satan. Look at verses 9 and 10. How does Paul describe 'the man of lawlessness' and what he will do? Despite all the uncertainties around Paul's

meaning, the one thing beyond doubt is that Jesus will defeat this man (v 8).

Verses 1 and 2 remind the Thessalonians that those who believe the lies of 'the man of lawlessness', live in the dark and take pleasure in wickedness will also be defeated by Jesus.

Don't let anyone deceive you in any way, for that day will not come until the rebellion occurs and the man of lawlessness is revealed, the man doomed to destruction.

**2 Thessalonians 2:3**

**RESPOND**
Jesus is light and defeats the darkness once and for all. Ask him to help you to hold on to that. Pray for people you know who are struggling with darkness at this time.

· · · · · · · · · · · · · · · · · · · · · · · · · · · · · · · · · · · · · · · · · ·

**Bible in a year:** Ezekiel 42,43; 1 John 2

## Friday 22 November
2 Thessalonians 2:13 – 3:5

# Stand firm and pray

## PREPARE
Read 2 Thessalonians 3:5. Make Paul's prayer your own as you spend time with the Lord.

...................................................................................................

## READ
**2 Thessalonians 2:13 – 3:5**

## EXPLORE
In verses 2:13–15 Paul thanks God for the Thessalonians. He comforts them in the face of opposition by reminding them of their identity in Christ (vs 13,14). Paul calls them 'first fruits' as they were the first to follow Jesus in Thessalonica. Because they are loved and chosen by God, they are to stand firm (v 15). Think about how these verses encourage you.

Paul prays that they would be strengthened by God (vs 16,17). Notice how Paul describes God (v 16). It is because of who God is that Paul is able to pray in faith (v 17).

In chapter 3 Paul asks the Thessalonians to pray for him (vs 1–5), that as he spreads the message of Jesus, others will come to faith, just as they did (v 1). He asks them to pray that he and his co-workers will be protected from opposition (v 2).

In verses 3–5 Paul is concerned for the Thessalonians. He reminds them that, despite the shaming and opposition by others, the Lord is faithful and they are in his care. Given their circumstances, how might Paul's prayer in verse 5 have helped them?

## But the Lord is faithful, and he will strengthen you and protect you from the evil one.
**2 Thessalonians 3:3**

---

### RESPOND
Pray for Christians around the world who are persecuted for their faith. Pray that they will stand firm (2:15); that the Lord will encourage them (2:15,16); that they are delivered from persecution (v 2); and that the faithful Lord will strengthen and protect them (v 3).

---

**Bible in a year:** Ezekiel 44,45; Psalms 129–131

# Work hard and take note

## PREPARE
Think about a time when your church community was disrupted by gossips. How did the church leaders overcome it?

...........................................................................................

## READ
2 Thessalonians 3:6–18

## EXPLORE
Paul's warning against idle troublemakers (vs 6–10) is stern. They are not following his teaching on work and community life. He implies that they have no excuse because he and his co-workers provided them with the model of how Christians should work and live (vs 7–9). Paul even gave them a specific rule (v 10). He is not addressing those who were unable to work, but those who were able and chose not to, expecting others to support them.

Paul says in verses 11–15 that the idle have become busybodies, becoming disruptive in the church's life by spreading gossip. Look at the balance he strikes in dealing with them (vs 14,15). The Thessalonians must avoid associating with these idle busybodies in order to cause them to feel ashamed (v 14). At the same time, they must not treat them as enemies, but should warn them with a view to the idle members being back in fellowship.

Paul concludes his second letter to the Thessalonians (vs 16–18) with a final prayer that they may know the peace of the Lord 'at all times and in every way' (v 16). Despite their trials and opposition, the Lord Jesus will be victorious. Those who trust God will find peace, rest and grace.

Now may the Lord of peace himself give you peace at all times and in every way. The Lord be with all of you.

**2 Thessalonians 3:16**

## RESPOND
Pray for yourself, that in all you do the example of Christ will shine through. Pray for your church community that it is not disrupted by gossips and quarrellers.

...........................................................................................

**Bible in a year:** Ezekiel 46,47; 1 John 3

# A bird's-eye view

## PREPARE
Imagine you are high up looking down on the area where you live. What do you see? Ask the Lord to speak to you today.

## READ
**Psalm 14**

## EXPLORE
This psalm condemns the arrogant – people who live as if God does not exist. The fools (v 1) are wicked and arrogant, not ignorant. The fools' arrogance results in them behaving badly through corruption and 'vile deeds' (v 1). The consequence of the fools' way of life is that God's people are abused (v 4) and the poor taken advantage of (v 6). Looking at our world today, we see that nothing much has changed.

In contrast, the psalmist identifies the benefits of believing in God and living as he wants his people to live. He affirms that God reigns (v 2). He recognises how few people seek him (vs 2,3). Contrary to what the fools think, he does dwell with his people (v 5). He rescues the poor and provides a refuge for them (v 6) and promises to restore his people (v 7).

We also see in this psalm hints about the Messiah (Jesus) who is to come from Zion to save and restore his people (v 7). Verse 3 tells us how much the world needs this (see Romans 3:23,24).

The LORD looks down from heaven on all mankind to see if there are any who understand, any who seek God.

**Psalm 14:2**

## RESPOND
Look at the news headlines in your area. Notice the indicators of people living as if God does not exist. Pray for God to reign in your local area. Pray for your church community that you will play your part in witnessing to a different way to live.

**Bible in a year:** Ezekiel 48; 1 John 4

# 'One flesh' fleshed out

**About the writer**
**Tanya Ferdinandusz**

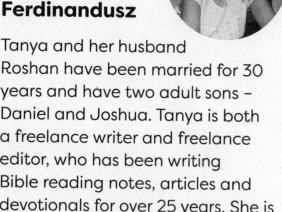

Tanya and her husband Roshan have been married for 30 years and have two adult sons – Daniel and Joshua. Tanya is both a freelance writer and freelance editor, who has been writing Bible reading notes, articles and devotionals for over 25 years. She is a Bible study leader and also works with couples who are preparing for marriage. She is the author of *Marriage Matters,* a book for Christian couples.

The superlative 'Song of Songs' (v 1) conveys the idea of most excellent. Of Solomon's multiplicity of songs, this song is the undisputed chart-topper that made it to the canon of scripture!

Controversy and confusion surround this song. It is unashamedly erotic. Its imagery is enigmatic. There's a single obscure reference to God (8:6). So, we wonder, what's this book doing in the Bible? 'All Scripture … is useful for teaching, rebuking, correcting and training in righteousness' (2 Timothy 3:16). This song is no exception. After declaring that everything he created was 'very good' (Genesis 1:31) and human aloneness was 'not good' (Genesis 2:18), God devised a one-flesh relationship designed for delight (just read Adam's love song: Genesis 2:23) and intended to reflect his own love-relationship with his people. In the world, sexual freedom is the norm; in the church, tragically, sex is sometimes viewed as being somehow less than spiritual. The song restores a much-needed balance about God's good design for sex, demonstrating the power and beauty of being naked and not ashamed (see Genesis 2:25), while promoting responsible stewardship of our sexuality.

Through the love story of Solomon and his Shulammite bride – their courtship, wedding, honeymoon and later years of marriage – the delightful details of what this one-flesh union might look like are fleshed out. 'Enjoy life with your wife, whom you love' (Ecclesiastes 9:9). In the song, Solomon does just that. And indeed, it is very good!

# Flourishing love

## PREPARE

'Christ's love makes the church whole. His words evoke her beauty. Everything he does and says is designed to bring the best out of her … that is how husbands ought to love their wives' (Ephesians 5:26,27, *The Message*). Who brings out the best in you?

## READ
**Song of Songs 1:1 – 2:7**

## EXPLORE

Notice the crackling chemistry between this couple! She longs for his kisses (1:2) and is 'faint with love' (2:5); he finds his 'darling' absolutely 'beautiful' (v 15) – as desirable as a solitary mare among Pharaoh's stallions (v 9). But there's more than attraction at work here. There's mutual admiration and appreciation: his name – representing character – 'is like perfume poured out' (1:3); her 'eyes are doves', which might signify a 'beautiful personality'.* This relationship extends from chemistry to character.

There's also public pride. This couple are happy and proud to be seen together: 'let his banner over me be love' (2:4). And within this secure circle of commitment, this young woman dares to confess self-doubts and insecurities to her royal fiancé (2:1). He responds lovingly, building up his beloved with sensitivity and commendable creativity (2:2).

Desire burns strong as this couple eagerly anticipate greater intimacy (1:4a; 2:5,6). Yet, they remain respectful of God's boundaries, keenly aware of the need for restraint, as implied by the repeated caution: 'do not arouse or awaken love until it so desires' (2:7; 3:5; 8:4). Love flourishes as it trusts in God's timing.

… do not arouse or awaken love until it so desires.

**Song of Songs 2:7**

## RESPOND
Reflecting on your relationships at church and beyond, what do character and commitment look like? Are there boundaries which need revisiting?

*GL Carr, *The Song of Solomon*, IVP, 2003, p86

**Bible in a year:** Daniel 1–3; Psalms 132–134

# Tuesday 26 November
## Song of Songs 2:8 – 3:11

# Marriage planners

## PREPARE
Wedding planners abound. But have you ever wondered why we don't also have 'marriage planners'?

........................................................................................

## READ
**Song of Songs 2:8 – 3:11**

## EXPLORE
Today's passage culminates with a wedding (6–11). Solomon's mighty warriors are present, along with the daughters of Jerusalem. Elaborate arrangements have been made. Clearly, much time, thought, resources and energy have been invested in ensuring that every detail is taken care of so that this 'day his heart rejoiced' (3:11) would be perfect!

Some couples prepare enthusiastically, even extravagantly, for their wedding day, yet fail to do the same for a lifetime of marriage. But this couple, in the lead-up to their wedding, also prepare diligently for marriage. Verbs like 'listen', 'look', 'arise', 'come', 'show', 'catch' and 'turn' (2:8,10,13,14,17) describe them being intentional about spending quality time together and daring to address difficulties. Coming out of our 'hiding-places' to show and share our true selves (v 14a) involves a risky level of truth-telling. Stripped of our masks, we stand 'naked' – and become vulnerable to 'shame' (Genesis 2:25). But as Timothy Keller says, 'To be loved but not known is comforting but superficial. To be known and not loved is our greatest fear. But to be fully known and truly loved is, well, a lot like being loved by God.'*

Listening ears and an affirming heart (v 14) foster trust and transparency. Within this safe space, couples must also proactively 'catch ... the little foxes' – those little problems – before they escalate and ruin their relationship (2:15).

> ... show me your face, let me hear your voice; for your voice is sweet, and your face is lovely.
>
> **Song of Songs 2:14**

## RESPOND
How might your local church facilitate more meaningful marriage preparation for couples?

*T Keller, *The Meaning of Marriage*, Hodder and Stoughton, 2011

........................................................................................

**Bible in a year:** Daniel 4,5; 1 John 5

# Drunk with delight

## PREPARE
**Reflect: What or who is beautiful to you? What sort of language do you use to describe beauty?**

## READ
**Song of Songs 4:1 – 5:1**

## EXPLORE

Every bride is beautiful on her wedding day! While the imagery describing the bride (1–7) sounds bizarre to modern ears – hair like goats, neck like a tower! – these images are book-ended by affirmations about her beauty (4:1a,7). In Hebrew thought, 'seven' symbolised perfection or completeness. As the groom's eyes move slowly down her body, mention of seven aspects – eyes, hair, teeth, lips/mouth, temples, neck, breasts – emphasises that he finds her 'altogether beautiful' (4:7).

After praising the wonders of her body, the groom initiates sexual intimacy – symbolised by the image of a 'garden' containing all manner of pleasing plants and exotic spices (4:12–15). Here, for the first time, he calls her 'my bride' – a phrase said six times (4:8–12; 5:1). Before the wedding, this garden was 'locked' (v 12); there was a level of intimacy that was out of bounds: 'Do not arouse or awaken love…' (2:7; 3:5). But now, it is right to 'awake[n]' love (v 16)! The bride, earlier veiled (4:1), is unveiled before her husband and responds eagerly to his invitation, without a hint of shyness or shame (v 16). Their union is deeply satisfying (5:1). The closing invitation is, literally, 'drink your fill of love' (5:1). While the Bible frowns on intoxication, this intoxication is God-endorsed: 'May you ever be intoxicated with her love' (Proverbs 5:19).

Eat, friends, and drink; drink your fill of love.

**Song of Songs 5:1**

## RESPOND
How can your church help all believers, married or unmarried, to 'honor marriage, and guard the sacredness of sexual intimacy between wife and husband' (Hebrews 13:4, *The Message*)?

**Bible in a year:** Daniel 6,7;  2 John

# Thursday 28 November
## Song of Songs 5:2 – 6:3

# Dealing with distance

## PREPARE
**Talk to God about a strained love relationship or friendship.**

. . . . . . . . . . . . . . . . . . . . . . . . . . . . . . . . . . . . . . . . . . . . . . . . . . . . . . . . . . . . .

## READ
**Song of Songs 5:2 – 6:3**

## EXPLORE

When the honeymoon is over, life's realities take over! He gets home late at night – perhaps royal duties had delayed him. But although he is eager to reconnect (5:2), she's grown tired of waiting and her greeting is cold (5:3). By the time better sense prevails, he has withdrawn (vs 5,6). There's not merely physical distance but a painful emotional chasm between the couple.

In the best of marriages, seasons of distance are inevitable, and it takes intentionality and effort to rekindle closeness. The young wife reaches out to the daughters of Jerusalem (v 8). True friends will never be complicit in a run-down-your-spouse rant! These friends' searching questions compel the wife to reflect on what makes her beloved so special (v 9). Her recounting of his charms (vs 10–16) closely parallels his description of her on their wedding night (4:1–7). He had said, 'You are altogether beautiful'; she now affirms, 'He is altogether lovely' (v 16). She also affirms the deep friendship that underlies their relationship (v 16). In the natural ebb and flow of feelings, a solid friendship between a couple can steer and steady their marriage through varying seasons. Finally, she reaffirms the bedrock commitment on which their marriage is built: 'I am my beloved's and my beloved is mine' (6:3; compare 2:16).

> ## This is my beloved, this is my friend …
> **Song of Songs 5:16**

---

## RESPOND
How can we nurture and grow our own friendships? Think of a valued friend and recall the qualities you appreciate.

---

. . . . . . . . . . . . . . . . . . . . . . . . . . . . . . . . . . . . . . . . . . . . . . . . . . . . . . . . . . . . .

**Bible in a year:** Daniel 8,9;  3 John

# Kiss and make up

## PREPARE
What's your conflict resolution style? Do you tend to attack aggressively? Ignore issues and hope they'll go away? Confront caringly?

## READ
**Song of Songs 6:4 – 7:9a**

## EXPLORE
The conflict (see yesterday's note) is on its way to a successful resolution. Solomon reaffirms how special this woman is to him (6:4,9; 7:6) but, despite using language reminiscent of the wedding night, he initially avoids mention of her lips, neck or breasts, with their more sexual overtones (6:5–7; compare 4:1–7). Since the rift was sparked by her rejection of his advances (5:2), this seems a wise move! Instead, Solomon focuses on her uniquely special place in his heart (6:8,9). Although her response is not recorded, it is implied that the couple were reconciled (6:10,13).

In the joyous process of making up, Solomon woos his wife with poetic praise. The seven attributes he had extolled on their honeymoon are now upped to ten – another number symbolic of completeness – although this time, he begins with her feet and moves up her body (7:1–5). Might the increased number of attributes and the more elaborate and erotic imagery represent deeper knowing and growing appreciation of his wife of some months (perhaps even years)?

Someone likened the engagement period to 'an exciting introduction to a dull book'. Solomon and the Shulammite would beg to differ! As they kiss and make up, it is clear that the excitement and delight of their dating days have not abated as they move forward in their journey of marriage (7:13).

> ... but my dove, my perfect one, is unique ...
> **Song of Songs 6:9**

## RESPOND
Pray for those experiencing disconnection in relationships.

**Bible in a year:** Daniel 10–12;  Psalms 135,136

# Saturday 30 November
Song of Songs 7:9b – 8:14

# Maturing love

## PREPARE
God uses the metaphor of marriage to portray his love relationship with his people (Hosea 2:14–16; Ephesians 5:31,32). How does knowing this influence your view of and attitude to marriage?

## READ
**Song of Songs 7:9b – 8:14**

## EXPLORE
During their courtship, the Shulammite had declared, 'My beloved is mine and I am his' (2:16). Early in their marriage, there's a subtle shift: 'I am my beloved's and my beloved is mine' (6:3). While still asserting that he is 'mine', the bride first affirms that she is her husband's, perhaps signalling a growing sense of security. Now, in the later years, love has matured. There's no hint of possessiveness, just a joyful sense of belonging and confidence that her husband finds her desirable (7:10), which emboldens her to initiate a romantic getaway (7:11–13)! Notice her desire to please her husband and her focus on giving rather than getting (7:12,13) – yet another sign of mature love, echoing God's 1 Corinthians 13 kind of love. To love well – freely, fiercely, unyieldingly, unselfishly – is to faithfully reflect our God who is the source of all love.

Looking to the end of the book, in the injunction for her beloved to make haste (8:14) the woman is demonstrating the same intensity of passion that we see at the beginning of the book. Reflecting on the use of the metaphor of marriage as representing our relationship with God, do we retain the energy of our first love like the woman still has for her beloved?

… for love is as strong as death, its jealousy unyielding as the grave. It burns like blazing fire, like a mighty flame.

**Song of Songs 8:6**

## RESPOND
Where and in what ways do you see signs of mature love in your church? How do you seek to maintain your passion for God?

**Bible in a year:** Hosea 1,2; Jude

# Doing life with God

## PREPARE
'Remain in me, as I also remain in you' (John 15:4). Are you letting Jesus remain in you? Are you taking care to remain in him?

........................................................

## READ
**Psalm 15**

## EXPLORE
This past week, we have traced the journey of a couple deeply in love. This pair were not interested in occasional visits; they were invested in a lifetime relationship with their 'beloved' and 'friend' (Song of Songs 5:16).

'LORD, who may dwell in your sacred tent?' (v 1) is not an application for a tourist visa but an expression of interest in permanent residence status! The psalmist was not seeking a casual relationship, but a happy ever after with his Lord! The items in the somewhat daunting list that follows (vs 2–5) are not prerequisites for this relationship – the Bible clearly states that we are saved by grace, through faith, and not by works (Ephesians 2:8,9). This psalm does not spell out admission requirements. Instead, it describes the character, qualities and conduct of those who have accepted the invitation to live with God. Since God's dwelling-place is 'sacred' or 'holy' (v 1), doing life with God involves desiring, delighting in and reflecting his holiness.

Despite being deeply committed, the Song's couple still had to engage in the daily and difficult work of doing life together – dealing with distance and disconnection, adjusting to differences and working through misunderstandings. As in marriage, doing life with God takes ongoing work and is not a point in time but a lifelong process.

LORD, who may dwell in your sacred tent? Who may live on your holy mountain?

**Psalm 15:1**

---

## RESPOND
How well have you been doing life with God? What areas may need special attention?

---

........................................................

**Bible in a year:** Hosea 3–6; Revelation 1

# Gospel grace for all

About the writer
**Peter Mead**

Peter is one of the pastors at Trinity Chippenham and a mentor with Cor Deo. He teaches at Union School of Theology and at the European Leadership Forum. He has written several books, including *Pleased to Dwell* and *Lost in Wonder* (both with Christian Focus). He is married to Melanie.

The book of Acts is the thrilling continuation of all that Jesus 'began to do and to teach' (see Acts 1:1). It is thrilling because we see the gospel spreading in the early years of church history. But it is exciting also because Jesus' work continues through people like us: ordinary followers of Jesus, empowered by the Spirit, facing opposition from society, and seeing Jesus' plan unfold to reach out from Jerusalem to the ends of the earth.

In Acts 1:8, Jesus gave the geographical progression of the gospel witness. It would start in Jerusalem, then spread through Judea and Samaria and to the ends of the earth. At the end of the first seven chapters centred on Jerusalem, persecution scattered the believers throughout Judea and Samaria (Acts 8:1). Now we come to the significant transition – moving the focus from Jews to Gentiles.

In Acts 9–12, we will find answers to some critical questions. Who will lead the charge in taking the gospel to the Gentiles? How will the followers of Jesus, with their Jewish background, be able to reach Gentiles with the gospel?

Let's dive in and see how God converts the church's chief persecutor, Saul of Tarsus. As Saul/Paul becomes the key figure in reaching the Gentiles, how will Peter, the key figure back in Jerusalem, become convinced of this Gentile mission? And what about Herod Antipas and his plan to destroy the apostles?

# The stunning confrontation

## PREPARE
Saul was young and zealous, a rising star in Judaism. Not only did he persecute followers of Jesus in Jerusalem, but he also sought permission to chase them across national borders. What would get his attention? How does God get your attention?

## READ
**Acts 9:1–9**

## EXPLORE
Saul of Tarsus was a young disciple of Gamaliel – a wise and moderate leader among the Jews (see Acts 5:34–40). But Saul was the rising star and wanted to come out from Gamaliel's shadow. A violent persecution campaign against the followers of Jesus would help young Saul make a reputation for himself.

What is the worst thing that could happen to the chief antagonist of the followers of Jesus? Surely it would be a personal encounter with the risen Jesus himself? That is what happened to Saul. As the bright light from heaven flashed so brilliantly that he fell to the ground, blinded, he cried out to ask who was speaking to him. 'I am Jesus, whom you are persecuting' (v 5) was not the response he could have anticipated!

It must have been startling to discover that all these targets for persecution who spoke of a resurrected Jesus were telling the truth! Saul was humbled and so startled that he spent the next three days without eating or drinking a thing.

> 'Who are you, Lord?' Saul asked. 'I am Jesus, whom you are persecuting,' he replied.
>
> **Acts 9:5**

## RESPOND
There could be no more stunning confrontation for Saul than encountering the risen Jesus himself. Indeed, there could be no more stunning confrontation for any of us. Imagine how you would respond if you suddenly met the risen Jesus!

**Bible in a year:** Hosea 7,8; Psalms 137,138

# Tuesday 3 December
## Acts 9:10–19a

# A different vision

## PREPARE

**Saul was blinded and alone with his thoughts in Damascus. He needed his vision restored, but more than that, he needed to know that there was a new and different vision for his life. Do you have a vision for your life?**

## READ
### Acts 9:10–19a

## EXPLORE

Saul could no longer be the rising star of Judaism, the chief antagonist of Jesus' followers. He had met the risen Jesus and that changed everything.

Jesus appeared in a vision to one of his followers, Ananias. He told him to go and restore Saul's sight. Ananias could immediately see the problem with this plan. He had heard of Saul's actions and authority to arrest anyone following Jesus – including Ananias himself. Danger lurked.

However, Jesus had a plan for Saul. He wanted him to see his new purpose: a God-given vision for his life. Saul would be the Lord's chosen instrument to proclaim the Jesus he had previously persecuted. And he would do that to Gentiles, their kings and Jews too. Saul did not have an easy road to travel.

Ananias followed the instructions. Saul received his sight and also the Holy Spirit. He was baptised, strengthened with food and encouraged by several days of fellowship with his new family.

> But the Lord said to Ananias, 'Go! This man is my chosen instrument to proclaim my name to the Gentiles and their kings and to the people of Israel.'

**Acts 9:15**

## RESPOND

Saul had travelled to Damascus to arrest these people, and now he spent some days enjoying being in God's family with them. Praise God that God's power can transform the most impossible case. Praise God that he could bring you into that same family as you trust in Christ!

**Bible in a year:** Hosea 9,10;  Revelation 2

# Rescuing a killer

## PREPARE
Have you ever seen a life so changed that the change was breathtaking? Not every conversion to Christ is so dramatic, but some are. Did people notice a difference in your life once you met Christ?

. . . . . . . . . . . . . . . . . . . . . . . . . . . . . . . . . . . . . . . . . . . . . . . . . . . . . . . . . . . . . . . . . . . . . . . . . . . . . .

## READ
**Acts 9:19b–31**

## EXPLORE
When Christ appeared to Saul on the road to Damascus, he changed the entire course of Saul's life. He had come to imprison followers of Jesus, but now he was preaching that Jesus is the Son of God. The change sparked antagonism from Jews that Saul would face time and again. They wanted to kill him and he had to escape town creatively!

Back in Jerusalem, the followers of Jesus were suspicious of Saul. After all, he was a persecutor and might be trying to trick them. Senior encourager Barnabas spotted the need and took Saul under his wing. He rescued the killer from suspicion and helped to launch a powerful ministry!

Again the Jews decided to kill this troublemaker, and again the Christians rescued him and sent him off to his hometown of Tarsus. The church grew as the disciples were encouraged in their witness, even without the new young evangelist in their midst.

> Yet Saul grew more and more powerful and baffled the Jews living in Damascus by proving that Jesus is the Messiah.
>
> **Acts 9:22**

## RESPOND
Often, a new follower of Jesus struggles to get going in ministry. Pray that God might make you a Barnabas – one who can spot what God is doing in a young believer and do whatever is needed to help launch that person into a life of effective ministry.

. . . . . . . . . . . . . . . . . . . . . . . . . . . . . . . . . . . . . . . . . . . . . . . . . . . . . . . . . . . . . . . . . . . . . . . . . . . . . .

**Bible in a year:** Hosea 11,12;  Revelation 3

# Thursday 5 December
Acts 9:32–43

# Quiet miracles

## PREPARE
It is easy to think of the more sensational miracles of Jesus. Is that how we think we should be representing him in this world? Or is there a key role to be played much more quietly?

## READ
**Acts 9:32–43**

## EXPLORE
The passage switches from Saul to Peter. In his travels, Peter was also able to offer spectacular ministry. Saul had been preaching boldly in the previous passage and now we see Peter healing a paralysed man. This miracle led to the spread of the good news through Lydda and Sharon. But not all ministry has to be so spectacular.

Luke introduces us to Tabitha (Dorcas) – a female disciple of Jesus with a reputation for always doing good and helping people experiencing poverty. When she died, Peter was called to come. The dead woman's life had made a quiet but real impact on the people around her. Now, Peter raised her to life in a way that seemed to fit how she had lived. He sent the onlookers out and quietly prayed. When he told her to get up, she did. It was a quiet miracle but it certainly had an impact.

Word spread, and many believed in the Lord! Every story in this section seems to end with an encouraging report of gospel growth.

> He took her by the hand and helped her to her feet. Then he called for the believers, especially the widows, and presented her to them alive.

**Acts 9:41**

## RESPOND
God does call some to spectacular ministry but praise God that he also uses the quiet and diligent service of others, like Tabitha. Just because something is quiet does not mean it won't have a vast eternal impact! What does ministry in your church look like?

**Bible in a year:** Hosea 13,14; Revelation 4

# The church is spreading!

## PREPARE
God intervenes directly to move the great story forward at critical moments in the story of Acts. The gospel reaching beyond Jews to Gentiles is one such giant step. It is so encouraging to see God's involvement here! Where do you see God involved today?

## READ
Acts 10:1–8

## EXPLORE
As we move to chapter 10, we meet Cornelius. He was a Gentile, an Italian centurion in the Roman army. Even though he was already connected to the Jewish people as a devout and God-fearing foreigner, it is still striking that he was actually a foreigner. (Of course, the Ethiopian official in chapter 8 was also a foreigner. Nevertheless, this is a significant moment.)

There is no sense that Cornelius' introduction to the story is a coincidence. God himself directly intervenes! He sends an angel in a vision. The angel encourages him that his prayers and offerings have not gone unnoticed by God in heaven. But now it is time for a new instruction: an active pursuit of a man named Peter. Cornelius jumps into action and sends for the man God wants him to meet.

God is often at work in unseen ways, working together the details of people's stories so that they can hear the good news for themselves. But sometimes, God works more overtly!

'Now send men to Joppa to bring back a man named Simon who is called Peter.'

**Acts 10:5**

## RESPOND
Whether or not God's weaving of your story was so overt, praise God for how he has worked in your life. Also, pray for God to directly call many more through dreams and visions, just like he did with Cornelius.

**Bible in a year:** Joel 1,2; Psalm 139

# Saturday 7 December
Acts 10:9–23a

# Newfound freedom

## PREPARE
Peter was a devoted follower of Jesus, and a faithful Jew too. How could this church leader get behind God's mission to the nations if he could not get close to Gentiles? How much of a change did Peter need to experience?

........................................................................

## READ
Acts 10:9–23a

## EXPLORE
In the previous section, we saw God taking the initiative with Cornelius the Gentile. Now we see God initiating with Jewish Peter. The Jew–Gentile divide was not easy to cross. Jews were trained throughout their lives to maintain their separation from Gentiles, strictly adhering to the purity codes of their religion. But now, a new message had to cross the great divide. God did not leave Peter to work it out. Instead, he gave Peter a timely lesson.

Peter saw a vision of a sheet lowered from heaven, with the heavenly voice telling him to kill and eat from the assortment of impure and unclean creatures (vs 9–16). What a shock this must have been to Peter. And yet, it was precisely the shock that he needed: a heaven-sent nudge to carry the gospel into Gentile dining rooms! With this newfound freedom, the gospel could travel much more effectively to the ends of the earth.

'So get up and go downstairs. Do not hesitate to go with them, for I have sent them.'
**Acts 10:20**

> ## RESPOND
> Are there areas of your life where you feel restricted from sharing the good news with others? Could this passage be a heaven-sent nudge to release you into sharing the gospel with more people?

........................................................................

**Bible in a year:** Joel 3;  Revelation 5

# Everlastingly safe

## PREPARE

Has there been a time in your life when you felt threatened or in danger? Perhaps that time is now. Call on God to protect you.

...............................................................................

## READ

Psalm 16

## EXPLORE

At the start of this psalm, David prays for the Lord to protect him (vs 1–4). He also praises God because he has seen God's goodness and guidance throughout his life (vs 5–7). It is always helpful to look back and recognise how faithful God has been in the past because it gives us confidence to trust him in the future.

So, in verses 8–11, David expresses his confidence in God's faithful protection. He anticipates that God will always keep him safe and secure (vs 8,9), and he is confident that God will never abandon his people, not even when they have to endure death itself (vs 10,11).

As Christians, we have an even greater perspective on the truths expressed in this psalm. We are confident in the face of death because Jesus has conquered death. David finishes the psalm with this hope-filled statement: 'You make known to me the path of life; you will fill me with joy in your presence, with eternal pleasures at your right hand' (v 11).

LORD, you alone are my portion and my cup; you make my lot secure.

**Psalm 16:5**

## RESPOND

In light of Jesus' victory over death, we can rejoice with Paul's great quote: 'Death has been swallowed up in victory.' 'Where, O death, is your victory? Where, O death, is your sting?' (1 Corinthians 15:54b,55).

...............................................................................

**Bible in a year:** Amos 1,2; Revelation 6

## Monday 9 December
Acts 10:23b–33

# Divine appointments

## PREPARE
Making an appointment can be complicated. You call a number, transfer to someone else and finally get the right person. Then you look for a time slot. What if God takes the responsibility for every evangelistic appointment?

.........................................................................

## READ
**Acts 10:23b–33**

## EXPLORE
In the previous two sections, we have seen God preparing Cornelius and Peter. Now we see everything coming together. Peter arrived at the home of Cornelius, where he found a ready-made audience to hear what he had to say to them. It was only ready-made from Peter's perspective. Actually, it was a God-made audience.

God's plan is for the message of the good news of Jesus Christ to be taken to the ends of the earth. That message – that Jesus was crucified, raised to life and ready to save anyone who will trust in him – is a message that God intends to travel. Indeed, we should trust God to make the travel arrangements for his message. What if God does all the work to set up divine appointments for his people to meet others and share what they need to hear? Does that not motivate us to look out for those opportunities in our daily lives?

'Now we are all here in the presence of God to listen to everything the Lord has commanded you to tell us.'
**Acts 10:33**

## RESPOND
We may not have visions of sheets and voices from heaven, but we still have a God who wants this great message shared with all households. Pray for God to give you eyes to see his divine appointments for you in the coming days.

.........................................................................

**Bible in a year:** Amos 3,4; Psalms 140,141

# A Gentile Pentecost

## PREPARE

God has done all the work to line up this moment in our passage. Now Peter will get to explain the good news to this gathering of Gentiles. What should he say? What would you say?

## READ

Acts 10:34–48

## EXPLORE

Peter was ready to proclaim Christ! He started by pointing to how God had brought him to that place. Peter went on to speak of what he had witnessed – the ministry of Jesus that God empowered, that Jesus was killed on the cross, but God raised him from the dead. Peter was an eyewitness and he was not hesitant to testify.

Peter proclaimed the facts about Jesus but also applied this truth to his listeners. He told how God appointed this Jesus to judge everyone. Still, anyone who believes in Jesus will receive forgiveness of sins. His message was good news if they would receive it. They did.

And just like at the church's birth in Acts 2, so here with these Gentiles the Holy Spirit came down upon them and they spoke in tongues. Peter had preached a message to them, but this sign was a message from God to him: these people are fully in the family, just as you Jewish believers are!

> 'Surely no one can stand in the way of their being baptised with water. They have received the Holy Spirit just as we have.'
>
> **Acts 10:47**

## RESPOND

Most of us are not called to be preachers, but we are all called to be witnesses. Are you ready to explain the good news of Jesus – both the facts and the application – for anyone listening? Our most incredible privilege is to point others to God's great news.

**Bible in a year:** Amos 5,6; Revelation 7

# Wednesday 11 December
Acts 11:1–18

# Ministry confirmation

## PREPARE
Take a moment to think about how God had worked to bring the good news to Cornelius. He had intervened with Cornelius and had to teach Peter a particular lesson. How did God bring the good news to you?

## READ
Acts 11:1–18

## EXPLORE
When Peter returned to Jerusalem, he was called to explain his 'unacceptable behaviour'. The idea of Gentiles becoming part of God's people without first becoming Jewish was a hard truth to grasp. The concept of Jewish believers like Peter going into Gentile homes was even harder to comprehend. So Peter told them the whole story (v 4).

The great confirmation of the story was the involvement of the Holy Spirit who had come on those Gentiles just as on the Jewish believers 'at the beginning' (v 15). The Jewish believers could not argue with Peter's story, nor with Peter's closing point. Indeed, God's people were now being brought together since the Holy Spirit is given to all who believe, whatever their background.

Even Gentiles were invited to repent and find life in Jesus – this was great and global news! Now there would be no limit as to who could receive the great message.

> 'As I began to speak, the Holy Spirit came on them as he had come on us at the beginning.'
>
> **Acts 11:15**

## RESPOND
Sometimes we secretly restrict God's good news. We may not say it out loud, but we might feel some people should not hear it or would not accept it. Imagine being with these believers and affirm again that the message of life is to be offered to all!

**Bible in a year:** Amos 7,8; Revelation 8

# Tying things together

## PREPARE

**Sometimes a story has numerous threads. There comes a point when they need to be tied together. Sometimes our lives feel like that! Praise God that he is more than able to keep track of every thread of our story.**

. . . . . . . . . . . . . . . . . . . . . . . . . . . . . . . . . . . . . . . . . . . . . . . . . . . . . . . . . . . . . . . . . .

## READ

**Acts 11:19–30**

## EXPLORE

At this point, the Jewish church in Jerusalem became convinced that Gentiles could receive the good news of Jesus by faith and be accepted by God. The Cornelius story had convinced them. But God's plan was for more than a few individuals to come to faith. Eventually, there would be churches full of Gentiles across the world.

It turned out that the gospel was already spreading among the Gentiles and a church had formed in Antioch. So Barnabas, the wise encourager, was sent to mentor them. He was encouraged by what he found and went to Tarsus to find Saul and bring him back to work together. They ministered in Antioch for a very encouraging year.

As Barnabas and Saul then travelled back to Jerusalem, they did so, instigated by the Spirit, with a financial gift to help with famine relief. So, we see the Gentile church reaching out in love to the Jewish church – a sneak preview of Saul's (Paul's) later efforts to unite the two groups with such gifts (see the third missionary journey in Acts 18:22 – 21:16).

He was a good man, full of the Holy Spirit and faith, and a great number of people were brought to the Lord.

**Acts 11:24**

## RESPOND

When Barnabas found the spiritual life in the Antioch church encouraging, he 'encouraged them all to remain true to the Lord with all their hearts' (v 23). That's a great prayer we could pray for ourselves and our churches today.

. . . . . . . . . . . . . . . . . . . . . . . . . . . . . . . . . . . . . . . . . . . . . . . . . . . . . . . . . . . . . . . . . .

**Bible in a year:** Amos 9;  Revelation 9

## Friday 13 December
Acts 12:1–19a

# Escaping death

## PREPARE
Some classic prison escape stories have been depicted in film over the years. Perhaps one of the most thrilling is this story in Acts 12. Prepare your heart to rejoice over God's rescue of Peter!

## READ
Acts 12:1–19a

## EXPLORE
In a passing remark, we learn that James, the brother of John, was put to death by King Herod. James was a key disciple in the Gospels and in the church's early years. Now he was gone and next it looked like it would be Peter's turn. Herod wanted a high-profile trial that would please the Jews.

The night before the trial, Peter was woken by an angel who miraculously led him out of prison. It became clear that God was not going to allow the church to lose two of its three key disciples in one fell swoop.

Peter, now free on Jerusalem's streets, headed for a home where the believers would be gathered in prayer. Perhaps this was the home where the Last Supper had been held; we cannot know for certain. But we can know for certain that God loves to answer the prayers of his people as they gather and cry out to him. Humorously, we are told of the servant Rhoda, who was so taken aback at hearing Peter's voice she forgot to answer the door for him!

> … 'Now I know without a doubt that the Lord has sent his angel and rescued me from Herod's clutches and from everything the Jewish people were hoping would happen.'
>
> **Acts 12:11**

## RESPOND
Peter had escaped death as the believers prayed. God does not always answer this kind of prayer with a 'Yes!', but let's join in with others now and pray for believers whose lives are under threat today.

**Bible in a year:** Obadiah;  Psalms 142,143

# Arrogance and worms

## PREPARE

God opposes the proud. Have you seen someone oppose God and set themselves up in God's place? Pride is a repulsive attitude to observe. Pray for humility in your heart today, even as you might pray for others who come to mind.

. . . . . . . . . . . . . . . . . . . . . . . . . . . . . . . . . . . . . . . . . . . . . . . . . . .

## READ
**Acts 12:19b–24**

## EXPLORE

Before the great story of Acts shifts focus onto Paul's missionary journeys in subsequent chapters, one loose end remains from the previous story: antagonistic King Herod. The heartless killer of the apostle James and would-be killer of the apostle Peter was still in power.

Luke explains briefly how a political spat with a neighbouring territory led to Herod's big mistake. He spoke in front of a crowd, who responded with excessive praise, calling him a god. The outcome was not ambiguous. An angel of the Lord struck him, and we are told that 'he was eaten by worms and died' (v 23). However that death sentence specifically worked, it was a humiliating and gory demise.

There is one God and he does not share his glory with any other would-be gods (Isaiah 42:8). It is always true that God opposes the proud but gives grace to the humble (1 Peter 5:5).

'I am the LORD; that is my name! I will not yield my glory to another or my praise to idols.'
**Isaiah 42:8**

## RESPOND

The passage, and our entire section, ends with an encouraging note. The word of God continued to spread and flourish. Praise God that his word continues to reach the ends of the earth, even today, despite all the opposition!

**Bible in a year:** Jonah 1,2; Revelation 10

## Sunday 15 December
Psalm 17

# The best place to hide

## PREPARE
What makes you feel unsafe? Some fear crime; others are more concerned about ideologies that threaten life as we know it. Whatever the threat, where can you go to hide?

## READ
**Psalm 17**

## EXPLORE
In this psalm, David makes three pleas to God. The first is essentially 'I am innocent!' (v 1); then comes 'they are attacking me!' (v 6); and finally, 'I am confident in God!' (v 13).

Notice the physical descriptions David uses. His attackers have 'callous hearts', arrogant 'mouths' (v 10) and 'eyes' intent on evil (v 11). He then adds an animal description: a 'lion hungry for prey' (v 12).

And yet, despite their calloused hearts, arrogant mouths and sinister eyes, David finishes this psalm expressing confidence in God. Why? Because just before these verses he has also given physical and animal descriptions of God.

Our God turns his ear towards us to hear our prayer (v 6), his authority is used to save his people (see the 'right hand', v 7) and his people are the apple of his eye.

This refers to the tiny reflection of the person in the pupil of the eye, revealing the focus of his loving gaze (v 8). And, like a hen, God spreads his wings to protect his people.

> Keep me as the apple of your eye; hide me in the shadow of your wings.
>
> **Psalm 17:8**

## RESPOND
The answer David anticipates is not focused on the removal of any threat. Rather, it is the anticipated joy of intimacy with God himself. What if God himself is the greatest answer to your prayer?

**Bible in a year:** Jonah 3,4;  Revelation 11

# In God's vineyard

From cries of distress (5:1–7) to songs of joy (12:1–6) Isaiah 5–12 is quite a journey. We get an insight into God's character, and the tension between his love for his people and his holiness, which cannot stand their wickedness and rejection of his ways.

Isaiah spoke into a situation of political upheaval. His call begins, 'In the year that King Uzziah died, I saw the Lord' (6:1). Uzziah had been king of Judah for decades. A modern parallel might be, 'In the year that Queen Elizabeth II died, I was licensed as vicar'. Isaiah locates his vision and call in a year people would remember: the year stability gave way to uncertainty and the growing threat from Assyria.

Except Uzziah's long reign had given merely the appearance of peace and stability. Under the surface things were not as healthy as they seemed. His death lifted the lid on the wickedness and injustice that had long been brewing. Isaiah was one of many prophets commissioned in those times by God to call his people back to faithfulness.

What he had to say makes us uncomfortable – but imagine how Isaiah's hearers must have felt! It's hard to read about God's anger, the reality of our rebellion and God's justice. Yet Isaiah had good news too: God (and no other) is our salvation (12:2), and he never leaves his people: 'great is the Holy One of Israel among you' (12:6).

About the writer
**Ben Green**

Ben is married to Jess, and they live in Birmingham, where he is vicar of Christ Church Selly Park and she is an A&E doctor. When he isn't vicaring, Ben is most likely to be found writing computer software, but he also enjoys walking up (real) mountains, playing the piano, and letting Jess plan their holidays.

# Cries of distress

## PREPARE
Have you been to a vineyard? Even if not, you can still picture the neat rows of vine after vine and imagine the careful cultivation, time and effort needed to tend and care for grapes.

## READ
Isaiah 5:1–7

## EXPLORE
You may recognise this parable – if not from Isaiah 5 then from Jesus' take on it (see Matthew 21). Those listening to Jesus would have known Isaiah's version, and also, first-hand, how hard it is to grow things – especially vines.

Look again at verses 1 and 2 and see the things the 'loved one' did to plant and guard his vineyard so he could make wine. No expense was spared, including buying the best grapes and finding the ideal location. He had good reason to expect an excellent crop followed by some delicious wine. But the result of his efforts is repeated at the end of verse 2 and in verse 4: was the crop what he had hoped for?

Reading about God's anger (vs 5,6) should make us uncomfortable. But this parable helps us understand why he was angry. Calling and forming his people wasn't only hard work; it was a labour of love. And he was rewarded with bloodshed and injustice (v 7).

> When I looked for good grapes, why did it yield only bad?
>
> **Isaiah 5:4**

## RESPOND
You are a vine in God's vineyard: the church. How has he lovingly and carefully planted and cultivated you in your journey of faith? Think back to some key people and moments, and give thanks to God for all he's done.

**Bible in a year:** Micah 1–3;  Psalm 144

# Tuesday 17 December
Isaiah 5:8–23

# God is... righteous

## PREPARE
How easy do you find it to receive criticism, be challenged over your behaviour or be told you need to do something differently?

## READ
Isaiah 5:8–23

## EXPLORE
When God gave his people the land, he was clear: it belonged to him (Leviticus 25:23). God's people were not landlords but tenants of his 'vineyard', hence the Jubilee when land that had been bought and sold had to be returned to the original family.

Here we have the people being greedy (v 8), living contrary to God's Law. Implicit in this is taking advantage of the poor: then, as now, it's easier for the rich to get even richer. The ungodly behaviour continues in verses 11, 12, 22 and 23, which paint an unflattering picture of God's people. But it gets worse: they are mocking God (vs 18,19). And it gets even worse still: they call evil 'good', darkness 'light' and bitter 'sweet' (v 20).

Isaiah is faced with a people who act wickedly and compound their sin by redefining God's way, so they are justified as right – and think they are so clever in doing it (v 21)!

Given all this, do you think God is justified in pronouncing 'woe' on such people? Do you agree with verse 16?

But the LORD Almighty will be exalted by his justice, and the holy God will be proved holy by his righteous acts.

**Isaiah 5:16**

## RESPOND
Invite the Holy Spirit to open your eyes to see where your behaviour is contrary to God's way, where you are justifying yourself instead of listening to God. Say sorry and ask him to help you change.

**Bible in a year:** Micah 4,5;  Revelation 12

# God is... angry

## PREPARE

**When was the last time you got cross? I mean really angry, with a passion that 'burned'? What caused it? Was it justified or did you go too far? What happened afterwards?**

## READ

**Isaiah 5:24–30**

## EXPLORE

This passage begins 'therefore' (repeated in v 25). How does verse 24 sum up the litany of wickedness we read yesterday in verses 8–23?

Isaiah tells the people: there will be consequences for your actions. We cannot do whatever we want and get away with it – for a while maybe, but not for ever. Isaiah gives two pictures of what those consequences will look like (v 24). I once put a couple of holly bushes and an old Christmas tree on a bonfire. Within seconds they caught and the fire was so ferocious the flames reached higher than the roof of our house. Rot is much slower and harder to spot, but no less destructive in the end.

Rejecting God's laws may result in the swift destruction of an invading army (vs 26–30) or the slow moral decay that destroys by hollowing out. And yet, do you see how warning his people through Isaiah is a sign of God's grace and patience?

> ... for they have rejected the law of the LORD Almighty and spurned the word of the Holy One of Israel. Therefore the LORD's anger burns against his people...
>
> **Isaiah 5:24,25**

## RESPOND

In verse 26 God whistles for Assyria like we might whistle for a dog. How might that vivid picture of God's sovereignty encourage you to pray for the situations (and people!) who make you really angry? Spend some time praying about these things.

**Bible in a year:** Micah 6,7; Revelation 13

## Thursday 19 December
Isaiah 6:1–13

# God is... holy

## PREPARE
If you could choose three adjectives to describe God, what would they be? Why are these three adjectives particularly important or special to you?

. . . . . . . . . . . . . . . . . . . . . . . . . . . . . . . . . . . . . . . . . . . . . . . . . . . . . . . . . . . . . . . . . . .

## READ
**Isaiah 6:1–13**

## EXPLORE
Before his election victory in 1997, former UK Prime Minister Tony Blair said that his government's three highest priorities would be 'education, education, education'. Now you've read the passage and the seraphim's song (v 3), I wonder what three words you chose to describe God.

I get the feeling Isaiah struggled to find the words to describe what he saw: seraphim (literally 'burning ones'), smoke, the hem of God's robe and singing so filling the Temple that it shook (vs 1–4).

However, what matters most isn't what Isaiah saw but what he heard.

'Holy, holy, holy' (v 3) is more than simple repetition. It means something like 'most holiest'. 'Holy, holy, holy is the LORD Almighty' – and therefore so should his people be, reflecting God's character.

Isaiah knew how far they (and he) had fallen short (v 5). He was sent to warn them of that, to call them back to God, to repent and be healed – though God knew they wouldn't listen (vs 9,10). Will you?

> ... I saw the LORD, high and exalted, seated on a throne...
> **Isaiah 6:1**

## RESPOND
Read verse 8. Isaiah was willing to go, to be sent by God – even before he knew what God wanted! Reflect on the places God sends you every day – home, work, shops, etc. Wherever you go, how can you reflect God's holy character? Might God be calling you to something new, like Isaiah?

. . . . . . . . . . . . . . . . . . . . . . . . . . . . . . . . . . . . . . . . . . . . . . . . . . . . . . . . . . . . . . . . . . .

**Bible in a year:** Revelation 14; 2 Corinthians 1

# God is... trustworthy

## PREPARE

What is the situation of greatest danger that you have faced? It might be as an individual, a group – or perhaps even a nation. How did you feel? How did you handle it?

. . . . . . . . . . . . . . . . . . . . . . . . . . . . . . . . . . . . . . . . . . . . . . . . . . . . . . . . . . . . . . . . . . . . . . . .

## READ

Isaiah 7:1–9

## EXPLORE

I didn't know it at the time, but as a Westerner I was potentially in great danger. The previous week another tourist had been mugged and killed on the street we were on. My hosts told me afterwards, and the anxiety I didn't feel at the time came flooding over me, even though by then we were perfectly safe!

Ahaz – Uzziah's grandson – was king. A number of years had passed since Isaiah's vision in chapter 6. Unlike me, he knew well the danger he was facing, and it was grave indeed. War was about to break out between the mighty Syria and the northern kingdom of Israel, whose borders were only 12 miles from Jerusalem. No wonder he was inspecting the water supply to the city (v 3), one of the most vulnerable points in a siege.

Isaiah knew that the attitude of the leader affects the people, to encourage or dishearten them. That is why he told Ahaz to keep calm (v 4), trust God and 'stand firm' in his faith (v 9). Do you think he will?

> 'Be careful, keep calm and don't be afraid. Do not lose heart...'
>
> **Isaiah 7:4**

## RESPOND

Sometimes we can forget God is worthy of our trust when faced with the immediacy of danger. Think of a situation of danger or trouble you or a group you're part of is facing. How can you be a person of calm, faith and encouragement?

. . . . . . . . . . . . . . . . . . . . . . . . . . . . . . . . . . . . . . . . . . . . . . . . . . . . . . . . . . . . . . . . . . . . . . . .

**Bible in a year:** 2 Corinthians 2;  Psalm 145

## Saturday 21 December
Isaiah 7:10–17

# God is... with us

**PREPARE**
Sit quietly for a few moments, take a deep breath and then think about one thing you long for God to say to you today. If you have pen and paper to hand, why not write it down?

**READ**
**Isaiah 7:10–17**

**EXPLORE**
On 11 August 1999, I was 16 and excited by the solar eclipse. We were on holiday in France, where it was almost total. I remember the sudden cold as the moon covered the sun, and making a camera obscura so we could see it without looking at it directly. But what did I see? Did I see a total eclipse or a shadow of one?

Something like that is going on in our passage today. Is the sign in verse 14 about Jesus? Of course not. It's about the possible invasion of Judah by Assyria. And yet it definitely is. Matthew 1:23 says Jesus' birth fulfilled this ancient prophecy.

The young woman giving birth to a son was a sign to Ahaz that the danger Judah was facing would be over soon (v 16). But at the same time it was pointing to something greater: the deliverance of God in Jesus – just as the shadow I watched of the eclipse pointed to the *real* eclipse happening thousands of miles away.

> '... the virgin will conceive and give birth to a son, and will call him Immanuel.'
> **Isaiah 7:14**

**RESPOND**
What did you write as you prepared for today's reading? Take a look, then read verse 14. Whatever is going on, however you feel, the sign of Immanuel means God is saying, right now, 'I am with you.' How can that make a difference to you this week?

**Bible in a year:** 2 Corinthians 3;  Revelation 15

# Rewards of faithfulness

## PREPARE
Are you a faithful person? Most of us like to think we are – but are you? Do you keep secrets? Do you love others even when they make it really hard? Do you let God mould every part of you?

## READ
**Psalm 18:1–29**

## EXPLORE
Psalm 18 is above all a song of thanksgiving. Being honest, the first five verses describe how I have felt for much of the past 18 months. I suspect you may feel the same way: confronted by death, opposition and struggle, both internally and 'out there'.

What do you do when you are 'in distress' (v 6)? In those darkest times, where do you turn? What brings you comfort? This psalm reminds us of the truth that God is not only the right place to turn (we all know that), but the best place to turn (sometimes we forget that).

How do you feel about verses 20–24? It can be hard to read David's opinion of himself! Two things are going on here. First, he was, compared to others, genuinely holy, the man 'after [God's] own heart' (1 Samuel 13:14). Secondly there is a prophetic side to many psalms, as David speaks words true of Jesus – and us. For, by God's grace, the rewards of the true faithfulness of Jesus are given to us who are 'in Christ'.

## To the faithful you show yourself faithful...
**Psalm 18:25**

## RESPOND
This is a psalm of praise and thanksgiving, so why not spend some time doing exactly that? You may like to use some of the words of the psalm (eg vs 6,16,17,28), or your own words.

**Bible in a year:** 2 Corinthians 4; Revelation 16

# Monday 23 December
Isaiah 8:1–10

# God is... rejected

## PREPARE
What does a place of perfect peace look like for you? (Biblical peace is about wholeness and completeness, not necessarily silence.) Where are you? Who are you with?

........................................................

## READ
**Isaiah 8:1–10**

## EXPLORE
It was easy for me to learn to spell my name at school – there aren't many names easier than 'Ben'! I feel sorry for Isaiah's son Maher-Shalal-Hash-Baz (vs 1,3).

The sign of Immanuel in chapter 7 is better known than this one, but they go together (see the end of v 9). They point to judgement (the coming of the Assyrians: 7:17 and 8:4) and hope (God is with us: 7:14 and 8:8,10). But why?

The 'gently flowing waters of Shiloah' (v 6) – a pool in Jerusalem – are like the vineyard in chapter 5: they stand for Judah, kings of David's line, the rule of God himself. The northern kingdom of Israel has rejected all that in favour of other kings. God's judgement is to give the people what they have asked for: he removes his protection from them (see 5:5) which opens them up to the Assyrians.

Whereas God's rule is gentle like Shiloah, the Assyrians are a destructive torrent like the mighty river Euphrates flooding its banks (v 7). Israel is about to find out: rejecting God has consequences.

> ... this people has rejected the gently flowing waters of Shiloah...
>
> **Isaiah 8:6**

## RESPOND
Why do we reject God? Why are we so tempted away from him and towards things which do us no good? Spend a few moments in quiet asking God to show you how you reject him, and then picture yourself turning back towards him.

**Bible in a year:** 2 Corinthians 5  Psalms 146,147

# God is... mighty

## PREPARE
What are you afraid of – to the point that it affects your behaviour? Losing something or someone? What other people think of you?

........................................................................

## READ
**Isaiah 8:11–18**

## EXPLORE
The prophets had a tough time. Often God called them to tell his people things they didn't want to hear, at the most difficult times for God's people. But I think the hardest thing – for them, and for us today – is living among people with different values, different goals, facing and travelling in a different direction. It's hard because humans are made for relationships, so we don't like to stand out as different.

That's why God needed to warn Isaiah (v 11). The people were anxious and afraid, with good reason given the looming threat from Assyria. It would be natural for Isaiah to let his focus slip, to start sharing the people's ways and anxieties and fears (v 12). How do you think you would react, faced with the same pressures as Isaiah?

The tragedy of the next verses is that God is exactly what his people wanted:

a place of strength and holiness (v 13). But they have rejected him, so for them his might is not a rock of protection but a stone of stumbling (vs 14,15). How does Isaiah respond to God's warning (vs 16,17)?

> The LORD Almighty ... will be a stone that causes people to stumble...
>
> **Isaiah 8:13,14**

## RESPOND
Spend some time thinking not about the situation faced by the people, but about the danger Isaiah was in: giving in to the ungodly ways of the people around him. Do you need to heed the warning he was given by God?

........................................................................

**Bible in a year:** 2 Corinthians 6;  Revelation 17

# Wednesday 25 December
## Isaiah 9:1–7

# God is... light

## PREPARE
Deep underground there are places where there is literally no light at all. Your eyes do not adjust; you cannot see a thing. Have you ever been in a place of such deep darkness?

## READ
**Isaiah 9:1–7**

## EXPLORE
I was outside stumbling in the dark trying to find the bin, waving my arms madly trying to set off the motion-sensitive light. Eventually it came on. The garden was bathed in light. Instantly I could see to get where I needed to be safely.

Isaiah 9 uses various pictures to describe the wonderful future that awaits God's people, including the light of dawn (v 2), the joy of harvest (v 3), the shattering of burdens and oppression (v 4) and the removal of tools and weapons of war (v 5). These are not tweaks to make things slightly better. These describe a momentous, world-changing moment.

'To us a child is born, to us a son is given' (v 6). The birth of a child changes the lives of her parents – and maybe a few other close relatives – but beyond that, not much is different. Yet *this* child changes everything, not only now but for ever (v 7). We know this child has a name – Jesus – and today we celebrate the day his light shone in the world's darkness, the day everything changed.

> The people walking in darkness have seen a great light...
>
> **Isaiah 9:2**

## RESPOND
Jesus is both our friend and the glorious King described here. Some days we need reminding of one of those truths; some days the other. Whichever you need to hear today, give thanks to God for the wonderful gift of Jesus.

**Bible in a year:** 2 Corinthians 7; Revelation 18

# God is... still angry

## PREPARE
**Are you the sort of person who asks for directions and listens to warnings – or who carries on regardless? What about when the warnings come from the Bible and you don't want to listen?**

## READ
**Isaiah 9:8–17**

## EXPLORE
Roadworks outside our house closed the road, but the closure was hidden round a bend. So the workers had put up several 'ROAD AHEAD CLOSED' warning signs, but many drivers ignored them and ended up stuck, unable to turn around, needing to reverse and go back the way they came.

After the highs of verses 1–7 we come back down to earth with a big bump and a reminder that the greatness of salvation is required because of the great pride of God's people.

In human terms their efforts were laudable. I can hear their leaders talking up the process: houses built with mud bricks and baked in the sun would be rebuilt but with dressed stone, and fig trees would be replanted but as cedars (v 10).

However, this wasn't a natural disaster that requires everyone to pull together for the relief effort; this was a warning, a taste of future judgement, a call to the people to return to the Lord. Did they listen? No (v 13) – so worse is to come.

Yet for all this, his anger is not turned away...

**Isaiah 9:12**

## RESPOND
Draw a circle on a sheet of paper and write 'WARNING' inside it at the top. In the rest of the circle write something God warns you about that you often ignore. Ask God to help you listen. Keep the circle near where you pray to remind you every day.

**Bible in a year:** 2 Corinthians 8; Revelation 19

# Friday 27 December
## Isaiah 9:18 – 10:4

# God is... just

## PREPARE
If you were queen or king of the world, what laws would you pass to make the world a better place? (You can give your real answer because no one else is listening!)

## READ
### Isaiah 9:18 – 10:4

## EXPLORE
Regularly these days the news contains pictures of wildfires – often in Australia or North America – and the devastation they cause. These fires move with ferocious speed, consuming everything in their path. They are virtually unstoppable, even with the helicopters and fire engines of the modern Western world. Imagine the terror they must have held to Isaiah's hearers.

No wonder Isaiah uses wildfire as a picture of wickedness: it might start small in briers and thorns but soon sets forests ablaze (v 18). Greed is the next example: it can never be satisfied but gets worse and worse, until we end up (metaphorically) devouring one another (vs 20,21). God's judgement is to give them over to this wildfire of wickedness (v 19). His vineyard will be destroyed (5:5,6).

This awful punishment is a consequence of the wickedness of Israel's leaders who have been preying on the very people who most need their protection, even manipulating the legal system to benefit themselves (vs 1,2). Such rottenness at the top had then spread like wildfire through the nation, so no one could be excused.

## Woe to those who make unjust laws...
### Isaiah 10:1

## RESPOND
Whether or not you are actively involved in local or national politics, how often and what do you pray for the leaders of your area and nation? Use 10:1,2 as a starter to pray for them today.

**Bible in a year:** 2 Corinthians 9; Psalm 148

# God is... sovereign

## PREPARE
What's the longest time you've had to wait for something you longed for? Perhaps you're still waiting? I suspect patience and self-control are two of the hardest of the Spirit's fruits to grow. If needed, ask for God's help!

## READ
**Isaiah 10:20–27**

## EXPLORE
Yesterday we thought about the destructive power of wildfire. Fire can destroy, but it also refines. Here we see the outcome of the signs in chapters 7 and 8, with a devastating link to God's original promise to Abraham. Read Genesis 12:1–3, then re-read Isaiah 10:21,22.

This is an example of God's judgement and mercy revealed in the same moment. Isaiah insists the 'overwhelming' destruction decreed by God (v 22) is righteous (ie deserved, proportionate, demonstrating God's perfect justice) and serves its original purpose (to warn the people and call them back to God). Some – the 'remnant' – heeded God's warnings and turned back to him in repentance and holiness (vs 20,21); refined and purified by the fire of God's judgement, they knew his mercy.

Have you been through the Refiner's fire? It probably hurt, but how did you feel afterwards? What was the end result? Whether you are through it or in the middle of it, in his sovereignty God can and does use even awful situations to form his people in holiness.

## A remnant will return...
**Isaiah 10:21**

## RESPOND
Passages like this give us a glimpse of God's mercy and judgement working together, but ultimately it's on the cross that God finally resolves the tension. Read the passage again, picturing Jesus both as the one willingly receiving the punishment and as the true 'remnant'.

**Bible in a year:** 2 Corinthians 10;  Revelation 20

## Sunday 29 December
Psalm 19

# Commands of light

## PREPARE
**What's the best piece of advice you have ever been given? Not a tip or a trick or a life hack, but something that has made a real difference?**

## READ
**Psalm 19**

## EXPLORE
Theology often splits the way God reveals himself into two parts: 'general' revelation and 'special' revelation. This psalm captures both of them.

Verses 1–6 describe 'general' revelation. These are the things about God that anyone can discover, from creation or within themselves. David talks about how the wonder of creation declares God's glory, from the majesty of the stars (v 1) to the warmth of the sun (v 6). There are exceptions, but throughout history most people have looked up at the sky and thought, 'That's amazing. It can't be there by accident.' That's general revelation.

The thing is, God is much more than a powerful being who made some balls of gas. That's where verses 7–11 and 'special' revelation come in. This teaches us not only about God's power but his character. The sun doesn't teach us that God is holy, or what it means to live as his holy people – but the Bible does. This is why we need both, and it is behind the mission of God's people. Everyone can see the glory of God in creation, but to know who he is – that, people have to be told.

> The commands of the LORD are radiant, giving light to the eyes.
>
> **Psalm 19:8**

## RESPOND
Read verses 12–14 and use them to guide your prayers in response to what God reveals about himself, in creation and through the Bible. Give thanks to God for his revelation, general and special.

**Bible in a year:** 2 Corinthians 11; Revelation 21

# God is... Spirit

## PREPARE
When politicians get caught out doing something they shouldn't, their defence is sometimes 'I have the right to a private life' – that is, their private behaviour is irrelevant to their public role. Do you agree?

. . . . . . . . . . . . . . . . . . . . . . . . . . . . . . . . . . . . . . . . . . . . . . . . . . . . . . .

## READ
Isaiah 11:1–9

## EXPLORE
In 2023 the famous 'Sycamore Gap' tree in Northumberland, England was vandalised and cut down; all that remains is the stump. Sadly, this may be the end for the famous sycamore because when a tree is chopped down, the stump is little more than a trip hazard.

The leaders of Israel had led God's people astray instead of in God's way. For that, they faced God's justice, laid out in the song of the vineyard in chapter 5. Now there was little more than a stump where once there was a thriving tree (v 1).

Yet for God this is not a problem. From this dry, dead stump will come a 'shoot' that will 'bear fruit' (v 1): a leader unlike any other. His character will be formed by God's Spirit (v 2). He will be truly discerning, full of joy and respect for God (v 3), righteous and just (v 4) and faithful (v 5). And he will usher in a period of peace that fills not only Israel but the whole world (vs 6–9).

> The Spirit of the LORD will rest on him...
>
> Isaiah 11:2

## RESPOND
Do you struggle to pray, to think and speak godly things, to walk his way and not 'your' way? Even God's perfect leader – Jesus – needed the Spirit to live in obedience to God. Ask God to fill you afresh with his Spirit today.

. . . . . . . . . . . . . . . . . . . . . . . . . . . . . . . . . . . . . . . . . . . . . . . . . . . . . . .

**Bible in a year:** 2 Corinthians 12;  Psalms 149,150

# Tuesday 31 December
## Isaiah 12:1-6

# Songs of joy

## PREPARE
Write a prayer or hymn of praise, giving thanks to God for who he is and all he's done for us. It doesn't need to be in iambic pentameter or rhyme – simply heartfelt.

## READ
**Isaiah 12:1–6**

## EXPLORE
This section of Isaiah began with the song of the vineyard, a poem about God's disappointment and anger with his people for their unfaithful and unfruitful lives. It ends with a song of praise and thanksgiving that makes me weep with wonder and incomprehension. How can God still love his people, given all we've seen about our behaviour? For we now are little different to God's people then.

In place of God's anger, we are comforted (v 1). In place of fear is trust (v 2). God is our strength, our defence, our salvation (v 2) – the wells of which are deep and joyous. This is the song of the 'remnant', those who have passed through the fire of God's judgement, purified and made holy to be his people. For God's people then this meant geopolitical turmoil. What does it mean for us?

This holy remnant will finally fulfil the original mission of God's people: taking the light of God's salvation, his might, all he has done, to the nations (vs 4,5).

How might you take that mission into the new year?

'Shout aloud and sing for joy … for great is the Holy One of Israel among you.'
**Isaiah 12:6**

### RESPOND
Read verse 6. And again. I'm going to write it down and stick it somewhere I can see it because I need a daily reminder: God is great, he is holy and he is with us (me), *whether or not I feel full of joy*. What about you?

**Bible in a year:** 2 Corinthians 13;  Revelation 22